T0195562

S.N.A.P.!

"GOD IS ABOUT TO DO HIS THING"

Timothy Leigh Walker

authorHOUSE®

AuthorHouse™
1663 Liberty Drive
Bloomington, IN 47403
www.authorhouse.com
Phone: 1 (800) 839-8640

Published by AuthorHouse 05/07/2019

ISBN: 978-1-7283-0694-0 (sc)
ISBN: 978-1-7283-0692-6 (hc)
ISBN: 978-1-7283-0693-3 (e)

Library of Congress Control Number: 2019903966

Print information available on the last page.

Scripture taken from The Holy Bible, King James Version. Public Domain

CONTENTS

PREFACE

S.N.A.P.! "GOD IS ABOUT TO DO HIS THING" (Armageddon & Haymengog 7-7-7) is my third book that coincides with my first book *"Spiritually Circumcise Your Heart and Mind,"* and my second book *"Four Horns that Control this Earth Age."* The acronym (S.N.A.P.) stands for *Satan's Not About People;* I use this because all Satan wants is as many Souls to join him in the *"Lake of Fire"* right after the final judgement of God and then Eternity begins. In addition, *"GOD IS ABOUT TO DO HIS THING"* is because this world and time we live in is going to hell in a— meaning people's free will has not been in line with God's Salvation Plan. With that said, Ecclesiastes 1:9 (KJV) says "The thing that hath been, it is that which shall be; and that which is done is that which shall be done: and there is no new thing under the sun." The "Book of Ecclesiastes" is written for the Men and Women walking under the sun; Mark Twin said there are two important dates in a person's life: "when they a born and when they find out their purpose." Some if not, most people are fascinated with money and power that they are willing to sell their soul without even knowing it. For example, the United States being the most powerful nation on earth today is allowing anything under their law; Fora person's Civil Rights goes against God's Law, Will and Purpose for His Plan of Salvation for All Mankind. Therefore, the million-dollar question is: how long do you think God is going to allow the United States and other nations to do whatever they want and want to do that goes totally against His Word?

NOT LONG!

Therefore, I dedicate this book to my twelve grandchildren and all believers in God and Jesus Christ as their Lord and also for those who are curious about what I have written and or those who may want to prove me wrong. For all believers in God and Jesus Christ as their Lord and Savior I must elaborate on some topics because I think most "Believers" have not been taught the "Truth" of what God has said, because of the "Traditions of Men" and "Denominationalism." Because of these two things and along with some other smaller things will have them in "Satan's Camp" if they or You are here when the Sixth Seal, Sixth Trump, and Sixth Vail (6-6-6) becomes a reality. I believe most Christians are being misled and some of them God has put a "Spirit of Stupor" on them to believe a lie. Example: such as the misinterpretation of Matthew 24: 40 (KJV) "Then there will be two men in the field; one will be taken, and one will be left." Most churches teach that the one taken is "Rapture" out of here by Jesus; and that's a lie straight from the pit of hell and one of Satan's main line/saying he will use on his arrival–"I come to rapture you out of here." Another truth that has not been taught from the Bible that might lesson all the racism and tension we have between people today is Genesis 1: 26-31 (KJV); God created "ALL THE RACES" on the 6th day and the "our" part in that verse is not God, Jesus and the Holy Spirit, but it is referring to God as "Elohim and His Angels" (You and I) when we were in our spiritual bodies. The Adam in Genesis 2: 5-7 (KJV) is Mankind (Ha-adam) and God did not have a man to till the ground as told in verse (5) and He formed "The Man Adam" (eth-ha-adam) on the 8th day and whom Jesus Christ would come through. For those who are curious and or may want to prove me wrong, I promise you will learn while trying to do so, because you will have to dig deep into the Bible (Word of God) and while doing so - learning will open their eyes and mind to Truth (s) that will change lives forever. The studying materials I have used to strengthen my Belief, Faith and Conclusions for writing such things that I think are very important in these Last Days. For my twelve grandchildren, my Prayer is "that they all come to know God for themselves so they can strive for His Divine Perfection by way of Jesus Christ. In addition, while they grow into the age of accountability may God's Shekinah Glory cover them and His Holy Spirit touches their parents to live and walk for Him, so they can be that Living example that they will need to Stand against the Wilds and Wickedness that are before them."

Notes

The number twelve (12) in Biblical and Spiritual perspectives for numbers denotes Government Perfection! It is the number or factor of all numbers connected with government: whether by Tribes or Apostles, or in measurements of time, or in things which have to do with government in the heavens and the earth. I am grateful for all my grandchildren and I have the responsibility to each of them and their parents to help them achieve the Biblical and Spiritual perspectives that has been expressed above and throughout the Bible.

One other great significance of this book is that it's my third book and the number three (3) Biblically and Spiritually means Completeness, though to a lesser degree than the number 7; but it derives from the fact that it's the first of four spiritually perfect numerals (the others being 7, 10 and 12). To give you more spiritual insight of the number 3; the three righteous before the "Flood" were Abel, Enoch and Noah: after the deluge there were the righteous "Fathers" Abraham, Isaac and Jacob (sometimes called Israel) depending on the situation, and there are 27 Books in the New Testament (3×3×3) or Completeness to the third power (3^3).

Jesus prayed three times in the Garden of Gethsemane before His arrest and those prayers are "The Lord's Prayer" that has Great Significance of God's (7-7-7). Jesus was placed on the cross at the third hour of day (9 a.m.) and died at the ninth hour (3 p.m.). There was three hours of darkness that covered the land while Jesus was suffering on the cross from the "6th Hour to the 9th Hour." Three is also the number of Resurrection and the Trinity/Godhead (Father, Son & Holy Spirit); Jesus was in the tomb for three full days and three full nights, a total of seventy-two hours before being resurrected. Therefore, I have put great emphasis on this book because it is the third book and because of what I have written above and in my other two books. I have said many times before that what is being Preached and Taught has some Truths, but it's not enough because there's "NO SEALING" of the Mind and Heart for the people to STAND on for what's about to Come and Happen. The most important question that goes through my Mind and Heart is how many of God's Children are being

Sealed with the Unadulterated Word of God? Those who are Sealed will endure Satan's Lies & Mischievousness while playing Jesus and the Truth what Jesus Christ said in Matthew 24:13(KJV) becomes reality "But he that shall endure unto the end, the same shall be saved."

Notes

The Bible has many figures-of-Speeches, Idioms and Symbology's, therefore you must get a clear understanding of what the writer is trying to say and who he or she is saying it to.

INTRODUCTION

To get the full understanding and meaning of what I am writing and what God said in the Verses that I will present to you; there are certain tools needed and you must be Prayed Up. God in Matthew 27: 51(KJV) "And behold, the veil of the temple was rent in twain from top to bottom;" so you and I can enter God's Holy of Holy and take advantage of what's free (Salvation) to save our Soul. The certain tools at a minimum are the King James Bible (KJV) and Strong's Exhausted Concordance by Dr. Strong that breaks down the English word (s) in the (KJV) back to the originally language Hebrew and Chaldee in the "Old Testament," and Greek in the "New Testament."

Please try to prove me wrong for what I have written are "Truths or Falsehoods!" Make it personal because it is your soul, but be my guess to ask your Pastor, Elder or whoever; but remember only the Holy Spirt will lead and guide you to all "Truth" and those people whom you ask will not be there for your Final Judgement given by God. For my writings I use the "Companion Bible"- King James Version that has 198 Appendixes authored by E. W. Bullinger, "Strong's Exhausted Concordance," "Vine's Complete Expositor Dictionary" keyed to "Strong's Exhausted Concordance" reference numbers, Smith's Biblical Dictionary and The Interlinear Bible coded with Strong's Exhausted Concordance reference numbers by J.P. Green, Sr... I am not saying you must purchase these materials, because they are in your Public Library.

Not all Bibles are the same, some has been tainted, meaning words has been changed as some people will say to give a better flow of reading, but in reality it takes away from the truth and what I believe is God's Natural

Plan for All Mankind or as I like to say the BIBLE is the Basic Instructions Before Living Eternally. Just remember every word in the BIBLE is not God's Word, but are inspired by God to be written so you and I can learn a lesson and be aware that things have been tainted with for a long time. This happen because of Satan and his children through the Genealogy of Cain Genesis 4:17-22 (KJV) that are Kenites (sons of Cain) are always busy to change and or taint God's Word whereby the original meaning is watered down. In addition, regardless of the Religion, Satan's main avenue is through denominationalism with their "Traditions of Men" who gives their interpretations and those people who believe and live their lives so are being divided from the Truth.

I believe this is a very much needed book for God's Children to adhere to, because Prophecies are being filled little-by-little daily. God said He wants Watchmen (Men & Women) to watch with their Spiritual Eyes, Ears, Heart and Mind and focus on His Word, so they can Spiritually Discern what's being revealed before them. With that being said, a person must know what to Watch for and I'm going to do my best to give you what God's Word has expressed what to Watch for and how He will end this Earth & Heaven Age (Dispensation of Time) and "Rejuvenate" this world back to its Original State, known in the Bible as a New Heaven and Earth as stated in Revelation 21:1(KJV).

In addition, with more emphasis I write this book for Christians and Spiritually minded people who are in search for the deeper Truths of the Bible and God's plan of Salvation for Whoever Believes On and In Jesus Christ and wants to keep their Amour properly shined, so they can stand and faint not especially if they are alive when The Anti-Christ (Satan) shows up on earth with his Seven Thousand angles telling people he is here to Rapture (Fly them Away) which is one of Satan's biggest lies and taught in most churches for what I call one of the High Norms of the Traditions of Men, because most people believe what their Pastor (s) say or has said are truths. Just remembering that Satan knows what God has said, therefore he quotes scriptures with a twist on it that sounds good and if you do not "study to show thy self-approved before God" 2 Timothy 2:15(KJV) you will fall for his lies.

Satan has no shame in his game, he wants as many Souls to join him and his angles in the Lake of Fire at all cost and will not quit until you order him out of your life "In the Name of Jesus," and even then, when you think everything is good to go and let your guard down, there one of his angles is. Remember and never forget that Satan tried to use the Word of God (Scripture) against the Word born in the flesh (Jesus) after He was baptized and fasted for forty days & nights.

Notes

That was Jesus's probationary period before he started His ministry whereby the number forty denotes probation. Read Matthew 3: 13-17 (KJV) Jesus's Baptism and Matthew 4: 1-11 (KJV) Jesus in the Wilderness.

We are spiritually in the Fifth Seal of God's (5-5-5), then comes (6-6-6) before the great (7-7-7). The Fifth Seal is for Sealing God's Children with Truth so they can be disciplinant enough to withstand what happens when the Sixth Trumpet is blown and Satan shows up playing Jesus, but in reality is The Anti-Christ to work his Sixth Seal & Sixth Vail which will be non-effective toward a small group who has God's Seal. With, if you surpass that, then the (7-7-7) passes you on for God's ultimate plan Salvation of the Soul and Spiritually Reconnected to God just like it was before the Katabole - Overthrow during the First Earth & Heaven Age.

Very Important rules for English Grammar is that you must keep the Subject (s) and Object (s) in line with one another and the Article (s) that belongs to one, if not both; therefore, when referring to a verse (s) in the Bible to another verse (s), they must at least have the same SUBJECT to bring the Object to its fullness. In saying that, when teaching and or preaching God's Word do not scripture pull because it might sound good, rhymes, or brings a tickle to the flesh! A Subject does something, and the product is the object itself. In addition, paragraphs also have Article (s) they are important to know that nouns can be either count (can be counted) or non-count (indefinite in quantity and cannot be counted). Therefore, count nouns are either singular (one) or plural (more than one) and non-count nouns are always in singular form.

Enjoy Your Reading

and

Journey Towards Truth

&

Eternal Life

CHAPTER 1

BOOK 1 SYNOPSIS

This book was written to inform everyone that there has been and still is untruths being preached and taught in churches today, and if your spirit is not in touch with God's Holy Spirit, then you will be deceived. You may end up following (The Anti-Christ, Lucifer, Satan, the Devil, etc.) straight into "The Lake of Fire." For example, in pictures, Jesus Christ is portrayed as a White person; No person alive has seen Jesus Christ, and sure enough will not print Jesus Christ as a black person or a person of color as described in Revelation1:14-15 (KJV); "His head and [his] hairs [were] white like wool, as white as snow; and his eyes [were] as a flame of fire; [15]And his feet like unto fine brass, as if they burned in a furnace;" is that a description of someone who White? I will let you come to your own conclusion, but it is not how Jesus is portrayed in movies, pictures, plays and stories!

People out of ignorance do not read, therefore they believe what is presented to them through photographs, illustrations, or twisting the Word to fit their ideologies. Satan will come acting as "The Savior" regardless who you believe is your Savior according to your faith. I tried to create the flow of truths that will be of great help to prepare you for that Great Day that is to come, and it gets closer day by day. Jesus cannot come back until all prophecies have been fulfilled and taken place in the order in which God's Holy Spirit inspired men to write what is in God's heart. I believe if a person does not know what happened in the beginning, then he or she will not understand what is to come at the end. Therefore, I give you a very short synopsis of the "Sandwich," the "Two Pieces of Bread" are the (First Earth Age gone and the Third Earth Age to come) that holds the "Meat" (Second Earth Age) that we live in now of that "Sandwich" as a reminder!

Note

Genesis 1:2 (KJV) says "And the earth was without form, and void; and darkness was upon the face of the deep." Using the "Strong's Exhausted Concordance" to break down the Hebrew transcript it should read [And the earth became] {tohuw va bohuw} without form and void (vain, empty, wicked and confused wilderness) and darkness was upon the face of the deep." The earth became void, but God did not create it that way! Something or someone caused utter confusion to come upon the earth.

Proof

Isaiah 45:18 (KJV) says "For thus saith the Lord that created the heavens; God Himself that formed the earth and made it; He hath established it, He created it not in vain, He formed it to be inhabited: I am the Lord; and there is none else!" Lucifer, that covering Cherub (hierarchy of archangels)

I believe was that Darkness. He caused the destruction of that first world (earth) age.

Note

Archangels and Cherubims are the elite of God's creation of Spiritual Beings and will not ever be born of woman as the rest of us where. Lucifer (the great dragon, that old serpent, called the Devil, and Satan) these are names given in Revelation12:9 (KJV). The names give meaning to the rolls he played throughout the Bible. Satan was one of God's most Beautiful and Wise Son's that was made in the full pattern as described in Ezekiel 28 (KJV), but He became vain (proud and conceited) and wanted to be as God and sit on the Mercy Seat that was and is reserved for Jesus Christ. He pulled one a third of the sons of God with him and caused them to follow him, instead of loving our Father. In Revelation 12:4 (KJV) Our Father was so hurt by this, that He had a choice to either destroy the third of the Souls/Angles who followed Satan or destroy/ put to End that First Earth Age (Dispensation of Time) that was Spiritual.

Note

We now live in the Second Earth Age (Dispensation of Time) in these Flesh Body's and according to Genesis 6:5-7 (KJV) "And GOD saw that the wickedness of man was great in the earth, and that every imagination of the thoughts of his heart was only evil continually. [6] And it repented the LORD that he had made man on the earth, and it grieved him at his heart. [7] And the LORD said, I will destroy man whom I have created from the face of the earth; both man, and beast, and the creeping thing, and the fowls of the air; for it repenteth me that I have made them." Yes, God has a Heart! With that said there is nothing new under the Sun according to Ecclesiastic 1:9 (KJV) "The thing that hath been, it is that which shall be; and that which is done is that which shall be done: and there is no new thing under the sun."

The thing that hath been will be in the Third (Earth Age (Dispensation of Time); it will be as it was in the First Earth Age (Spiritual) again after {7-7-7, Millennium (One Thousand Years to teach of nothing but the Truth) and then Satan will be loosed at the end of the Millennium for a short season to test those who did not make the "First Resurrection." After that testing God's Great White Throne Judgement will happen and those who do not make the "Second Resurrection" will be blotted out by being thrown into the "Lake of Fire." Then "Eternity" will begin, and God will Rejuvenate the Earth and set-up His Kingdom right here on Earth Hallelujah!

God so loved His children that instead of destroying their Souls, God put His plan of Salvation into action to have every Soul beside His Arch Angles and Cherubims be birth innocent through the womb of woman is actually the First Baptism of the Soul in this Second Earth Age (Dispensation of Time) that is now of "Flesh." God passed sentence (Death of the Soul-To be Blotted Out) on Lucifer (Son of Perdition, Serpent, Satan, Dragon, Devil, Prince & King Tyrus, The Anti-Christ), *Abaddon* in the Hebrew tongue and *Apollyon* in the Greek tongue Revelation.9:11 (KJV). In addition, God passed sentence (Death of the Soul-To be Blotted Out) on Satan's "Seven Thousand Lieutenants" (Angels) after they refused to be born of woman and left their first estate as stated in Jude 1: 6 (KJV) "And the angels which kept not their first estate, but left their own habitation, he hath reserved in everlasting chains under darkness unto the judgment of the great day." They did so to seduce women that were a new thing God had formed from man's DNA, not Rib; and yes, they impregnated women, and that's how the Giants (Rephaim) came about in Genesis 6:4 (KJV) "There were giants in the earth in those days; and also after that, when the sons of God came in unto the daughters of men, and they bare children to them, the same became mighty men which were of old, men of renown." God wants His Men and Women to be Watchmen, therefore I am obligated to inform you that Satan in the role of the serpent had sex with Eve, and sometime afterwards Adam and Eve had sex.

First Norm

That the earth was created in six days as it reads in Genesis 1: 2-31(KJV) and then God rested on the seventh day Genesis 2: 1-3 (KJV) and then the generation of The Adam and Eve begins in Genesis 2: 7 (KJV) when God formed, not created! One important thing to note and understand the in English ligature the word "And" does not start a sentence as it does in Genesis 1:2-31 (KJV) and throughout Genesis 2 (KJV). The word "And" is a coordinating conjunction which joins words, phases, and clauses that are balanced in logical equals, but when it begins a sentence, it becomes a Polysyndeton the repetition of this conjunction word adds power to the other words, therefore letting the reader know that there is more into which you are reading so slow down and really comprehend what is written. In early Hebrew ligature there was no punctuations, so the interpreters tried to do the best that they could do without taking away the meaning hoping you would pick up on its importance's. The six days mentioned of creation as stated in Genesis chapter one I believe to be done in Years (One Thousand).

The reason I do not believe it to be literal days is because after reading other parts of the Bible; why did God say in Psalms 90:4 (KJV) says "For a thousand years in thy sight are but as yesterday when it is past, and as a watch in the night." The cross reference to that is in the New Testament II Peter 3:8 (KJV) "But do not forget this one thing, dear friends: With the Lord a day is like a thousand years, and a thousand years are like a day." Therefore, science proves the Bible that this earth is millions of years old and that the Sun is older and the center of this universe. In Genesis 1:16 (KJV) "And God made two great lights; the greater light to rule the day, and the lesser light to rule the night: he made starts also." That greater light is the Sun and the lesser light is the Moon! When God spoke in (Genesis 3 KJV) "Let there be light" God's Holy Spirit brought fought the earth out of darkness into His marvelous light.

Food for Thought

Genesis 5:27 (KJV) says "And all the days of Methuselah were nine hundred sixty and nine years: and he died." One can say that he and every human being will not physically be out of the presence of God for a full day according to His timeline. So put this thought to work in your mind that those six days of creation are Six Thousand Years, God rested for a Thousand Year and then formed The Adam (eth-ha'adham) whose genealogy He/Jesus Christ would be born through (become flesh by being born of a woman). Hum!

Second Norm

Genesis 1:2 (KJV) says "And the earth was without form, and void; and darkness was upon the face of the deep. And the Spirit of God moved upon the face of the waters." The word "was"$_{56}$ is (hayah) in the Hebrew language that means "became" and the words "without form and void" is (tohuw va bohuw) means vain, empty, wicked, and confused wilderness. God did not create the Earth "without form and void" and if you believe so, then the LORD lied to Isaiah. (Isaiah 45:18 KJV) "For thus saith the LORD that created the heavens; God himself that formed the earth and made it; he hath established it, he created it not in vain, he formed it to be inhabited: I am the LORD; and there is none else." Now that you have read that God did not create the earth void and without form there should be a question in your mind of why did the earth become void and without form?

Therefore, Genesis 1:2 (KJV) should say "The earth became vain, empty, wicked, and a confused wilderness." The reason is that Lucifer (darkness) that covering cherub caused such confusion when he convinced a third of the sons of God (angels) to follow him instead of loving their Father, therefore, he was kicked out of heaven and thrown (Katabole) upon the face of the deep/earth after losing his position as the "Covering Cherub" and sentenced to death as described in Ezekiel 28 (KJV). The reason that the Spirit of God (Holy Spirit) moved upon the face of the waters was because there was the Flood of all Floods and the beginning of God putting forth His plan of Salvation into action. Those words are a mouth full and maybe mind blowing for some that Satan/Lucifer convinced a third of God's angles to follow him. Let it be known that there is a great difference in (Followers & Elect); Satan has Seven Thousand Elect Angles and along

6

with him have no chance to obtain salvation and will be the first to be cast into the Lak of Fire. Therefore, God loving all His children decided to destroy that Earth Age instead of killing a third of His children set a plan into action to salvage their Soul that they too may have ever lasting life with Him in Eternity. Ecclesiastes 1:9 (KJV) says "The thing that hath been, it is that which shall be; and that which is done is that which shall be done: and there is no new thing under the sun." Therefore, after reading the scriptures below one can form their own opinion but remember to pray and let the Holy Spirit to lead and guide you. Satan rebelled and was cast out of heaven in the First Earth Age and he's in heaven held in chains behind Jesus Christ now during this Second Earth Age; but will be cast out again before the end of this age with his elect angles.

Isaiah 14:12 (KJV) says "How you have fallen from heaven, O morning star, son of the dawn! You have been cast down to the earth, you who once laid low the nations." When Lucifer sinned, Jesus said, "I saw Satan fall like lightning from heaven" Luke 10:18 (KJV), and in the Book of the Revelation Satan is seen as "a star that had fallen from the sky to the earth" Revelation 9:1 (KJV). In addition: that one third of an "innumerable company of angels" Hebrews 12:22 (KJV) chose to rebel with him. John saw this great wonder in heaven, "… an enormous red dragon… His tail swept a third of the stars out of the sky and flung them to the earth… the great dragon was hurled down that ancient serpent called the devil, or Satan, who leads the whole world astray. He was hurled to the earth and his angels with him" Revelation 12:3-9 (KJV). Since Satan is referred to as a star which fell or was cast down (Katabole) to earth, and Revelation 12:4 (KJV) says a third of the stars were cast out with him, then the conclusion is that the stars in Revelation 12 (KJV) refer to fallen angels, fully one third of the heavenly host.

Third Norm

When you read about Eve in Genesis 3:6 (KJV) "she took of the fruit thereof, and did eat, and gave also unto her husband with her; and he did eat." This is the reason there are two genealogies in Genesis, One of The Adam and one of Cain; therefore, if Cain was of The Adam, he would be in The Adam's

Genealogy, but he is not. Also, in that verse there are idioms and metaphors used throughout the Word of God and one must be able to discern and understand what God is really telling us. One thing is that there is no "Apple" mention, so that was not the fruit, but the fruit is the metaphor and men today used the metaphor (I busted that Cherry) especially if it's when a woman first has sex and bleeds, Hmm! Also, do not look over that "The Adam" also took of the same fruit that Eve fore took of; therefore, I believe that was the first encounter of homosexuality in the Bible.

A. "The Adam" and Eve "What really happen in the Garden of Eden?" Genesis 3 (KJV)

Before getting into what happen one must know why there was The Adam and Eve after God had already created men and women (all the races) on the sixth day. The reason for The Adam and Eve being singled out from the creation of the rest of mankind is because that through the womb of Eve, umbilical cord to umbilical cord, would eventually four- thousand years later, be born the Jesus the Christ.

The Bible is the story of one man's family and the peoples that they encounter through-out history. That is the history of Adams family, through which Jesus Christ would come. And through the sacrifice of Jesus Christ on the cross, all peoples from all the Nations (eth'-nos) in the Greek of the New Testament, & (gowy {go'-ee}) in the Hebrew of the Old Testament of the earth can be grafted into the eternal family of God in the eternity, in Heaven!

It was in His (the Lord God's) image that The Adam was formed, not created because in Genesis 1:27-28 (KJV) all the races of people where created on the (6th Day); 27 "So God created man in his own image, in the image of God created he him; male and female created them. 28 And God blessed them, and God said unto them, Be fruitful, and multiply, and replenish the earth, and subdue it: and have dominion over the fish of the sea, and over the fowl of the air, and over every living thing that moveth upon the earth."

Note

God did not say to them to have dominion over one another or people! In the New Testament Jesus is referred to as The last Adam and the reason for this is so that there would be a direct genetic lineage from God Almighty Himself, through "The Adam" and through Eve (whom God took DNA from The Adam to form her), through Seth, all the way down through successive generations, umbilical cord to umbilical cord, through which would be born Jesus Christ (who was from a virgin birth from God through Mary). Thus, Jesus Christ would be the perfect Lamb - without spot or blemish - the perfect and once for all time sacrifice, for the atonement of sins of all mankind! Jesus was 100% man and 100% God both Physically and Spiritually Genesis 1:26a (KJV) says "Let us make man in our image, after our likeness." I propose to you that was God as Elohim was speaking to His Angles (You & I) and we look as we do—but young with mortal souls unless we adhere to God's Salvation Plan (Salvaging the Soul) and become immortal souls.

This is also why Eve is referred to as "the Mother of all living," for through her would come the Savior of the World-Jesus Christ, and through Him all can live eternally. Many read that Eve was the mother of all living and confuse it to mean that she was the first woman. This is not so, the word Eve in the Hebrew language means: Mother of all living, the Bible interpreting it for you by saying "And Adam called his wife's name Eve; because she was the mother of all living." Genesis 3:20 (KJV). For Eve, and all other people could live eternal by the fruit of her womb, Jesus; hence it is written of Eve: "she shall be saved in childbearing, if they continue in faith and charity and holiness with sobriety" I Timothy 2:13-15 (KJV).

All the names in the Bible have meanings, and in understanding the meanings of the names in their native languages gives us a deeper insight into what the meaning of certain verses are. Look in a Smith's Bible Dictionary will supply the meanings (translations) of every proper people/person and place named in the Bible, read a review of the Smith's Bible Dictionary. Now, to the very interesting topic of and coming out the gate with it one must know what (beguile) means and being (seduced). If you do not get this straight in your Heart and Mind, then there is no way you will know who your enemies and why God said in Ezekiel 3:17 (KJV) "Son of man, I have made thee a watchman unto the house of Israel: therefore, hear the word at my mouth, and give them warning from me." We too are to be Watchmen and I am obligated to inform you that Satan in the role of the serpent had sex with Eve, and then Adam & Eve had sex.

Now before blowing me off and thinking I am crazy, thoroughly read Genesis 2 (KJV), because God never said anything about any Fruit nor Touch either Tree. God said in Genesis 2: 16 (KJV) "And the LORD God commanded the man, saying, of every tree of the garden thou mayest freely eat: [17] But of the tree of the knowledge of good and evil, thou shalt not eat of it: for in the day that thou eatest thereof thou shalt surely die."

The serpent went to Eve because God never spoke to Eve, and you know how easy it is to misquote that which was spoken to us by another person. Therefore, the serpent placed doubt into Eve's mind by saying in Genesis 3: 1-5 (KJV) "Yea, hath God said, Ye shall not eat of every tree of the garden? [2] And the woman said unto the serpent, We may eat of the fruit of the trees of the garden: [3] But of the fruit of the tree which is in the midst of the garden, God hath said, Ye shall not eat of it, neither shall ye touch it, lest ye die." Satan knew what God had told Adam, and that Eve had messed it all up, therefore the serpent (Satan) knew he could do whatever he wants to do and that was a lie: [4] "And the serpent said unto the woman, Ye shall not surely die: [5] For God doth know that in the day ye eat thereof, then your eyes shall be opened, and ye shall be as gods, knowing good and evil."

Note

Then in verse 2 Eve started misquoting what God had said because she heard it from Adam and not God for herself I know you are saying to yourself how did the author get that the Serpent (Satan/Devil) had sex with Eve; the word Touch[52] is Strong's Hebrew #5060 naga' (naw-gah); a primitive root; properly, to touch, i.e. lay the hand upon (for any purpose; euphem, to lie with a woman). The word beguiled in Genesis 3:13 (KJV) is Strong's Hebrew #5377 nasha (naw-shaw); a primitive root; to lead astray, i.e. (mentally) to delude, or (morally) to seduce: Strong's # 1818 exapatao (ex-ap-at-ah'o): from 1537 to 538; to seduce wholly. Do not miss this for God is speaking to Satan (serpent) and the word (seed) in Genesis 3:15 (KJV) in Strong's Hebrew is #2233 Zera and its prime root is #2232 Zara {conceive and or make pregnant} and #4690 in Greek σπέρμα is sperma (sper'mah) the male sperm by implication offspring. Genesis 3: 14-15 (KJV) says "And the LORD God said unto the serpent, Because thou hast done this, thou art cursed above all cattle, and above every beast of the field; upon thy belly shalt thou go, and dust shalt thou eat all the days of thy life: ¹⁵ And I will put enmity between thee and the woman, and between thy seed and her seed; it shall bruise thy head, and thou shalt bruise his heel." The last part of this verse is the first Prophecy given by God and only half has been fulfilled when Jesus was nailed to the cross!

Note

You should ask yourself why I used Strong's #4690 in the Greek language to fit my understanding that there was sex in the Garden, I am glad you asked! Because God said in Genesis 3: 16 (KJV) "Unto the woman he said, I will greatly multiply thy sorrow and thy conception; in sorrow thou shalt bring forth children; and thy desire shall be to thy husband, and he shall rule over thee." Satan knew that Jesus Christ was coming through the genealogy of The Adam and Eve, so he tried to corrupt that seed line in which Jesus Christ would be coming through; not only him by himself, but with his elect (7,000) angles who never was born of woman as mention in the Book of Jude. Jude 1: 6 (KJV) says "And the angels which kept not their first estate, but left their own habitation, he hath reserved in everlasting chains under darkness unto the judgment of the great day."

B. Genealogy of "The Adam and Cain"- (Two Seeds)

Genesis 4 & 5 (KJV)

Why in Genesis do we read that there are two genealogies, one of Adam and one of Cain? Simple answer is because Cain was not of Adam, but of Satan the (serpent) and that is why you do not read of him being in Adam's genealogy. Eve had fraternal twins Cain & Abel, and everyone knows that Cain killed Abel. It is a known fact that a woman can conceive from two different men or by the same man at a different time and have twins in one pregnancy. Therefore, Jesus said in John 8: 44(KJV) "Ye are of your father the devil, and the lusts of your father ye will do. He was a murderer from the beginning, and abode not in the truth, because there is no truth in him. When he speaketh a lie, he speaketh of his own: for he is a liar, and the father of it."

Be Watchmen because the names are similar!

Adam's Genealogy Genesis 5 (KJV) After Abel's death: Adam – begat Seth	Cain's Genealogy Genesis 4: 16-24 (KJV) Cain – begat Enoch
Seth – begat Enos	Enoch – beget Irad
Enos – begat Cainan	Irad – begat Mehujael
Cainan – begat Mahalaleel	Mehujael – begat Lemach
Mahalaleel – begat Jared	Lemach - begat Jabal & Jubal from his wife Adah, and Tubal-Cain from his wife Zillah
Jared – begat Enoch	
Enoch – begat Methuselah	
Methuselah – begat Lamech	
Lamech – begat Noah	
Noah – begat (Shem, Ham and Japheth)	

If you did not know it, Satan is supernatural and when he comes as Jesus, he will make things happen that only one would believe that God can do. In addition, he will have the biggest Revival the world has ever seen or heard of and that is the (Norms) for many teachings that will be manifested, so they will believe he is Jesus Christ. The Bible said that the whole world will follow him, and therefore Jesus said he would shorten the time to five months. Revelation 9:5 (KJV) says "And to them it was given that they should not kill them, but that they should be tormented five months:" because of the many roles Satan will play and he may even fool the Elect. Let us see what Jesus said, and remember He is not talking about the Soul and Spiritual Body! Matthew 24: 20-24 (KJV) says "[20]But pray ye that your flight be not in the winter, neither on the sabbath day: [21]For then shall be great tribulation, such as was not since the beginning of the world to this time, no, nor ever shall be [22] And except those days should be shorten, there should no flesh be saved: but for the elect's sake those days shall be shortened. [23] Then if any man shall say unto you, Lo, here [is] Christ, or there; believe [it] not. [24]For there shall arise false Christs, and false prophets, and shall shew great signs and wonders; insomuch that, if [it were] possible, they shall deceive the very elect."

Fourth Norm: Speaking in Tongues! Is it the Cloven Tongues or Gibberish?

I ask this question because we are approaching the End Times/Second Advent or I should say we are in the Last (Fig Tree) Generation in which our Lord Jesus Christ will be coming back, and if what is being taught and practice as Speaking in Tongues is not in accordance to the Word of God, then it needs to stop. I have asked God to show me in His Word about Speaking in Tongues, so what I want to do is share what has been revealed to me by God through my studies, and not Traditions of Men. The bottom Line and Question: Are You Speaking or is the Holy Spirit speaking through you? I read Acts 2; 10; and 19 (KJV) that it was the Holy Spirit that spoke through the people and it went out in every language for the listeners-even down to their own dialect. It was not the people themselves doing the Speaking in Tongues (Other-All Languages) when they felt it needed to be done or try to show others that they were filled with the Holy Spirit and say that they are speaking to God!

The issue about Speaking in Tongues is not worth you and I to fall out over; we can agree to disagree and still be Brother & Sister in Christ, but let's get this correct because it's a sin to misguide God's children.

13

According to the "Strong's Exhausted Concordance" of the "King James Bible" Greek #1100 - Glossa (gloce-sah') Tongues is a language (especially one naturally unacquired), and Greek #2084 -states other tongued, i.e., a foreign language. These two definitions are used as tongues in the New Testament of the Bible, and the listeners heard in their own language is Greek #2398 - meaning his own and in laymen's term dialect. On the "Day of Pentecost" there were no unknown tongue spoken, but it was unknown to the speakers that were being used by the Holy Spirit to speak with Cloven Tongues—meaning it went out in every language because the people that heard them speak were from every part of the earth there to worship. Also, man added the word "*unknown*" and all the words that are in "italics" in the "King James Bible" were added by man, so that the conversation could be carried on-thinking it would be better understood in English.

Gibberish or I can even say babel is a rapid nonsensical chatter, or a confused noise typically that's made by several voices. Remember I Corinthians 14:33a (KJV) says "For God is not the author of Confusion" and if an unbeliever or a Christian of little knowledge was to walk in a church and a person or people are "what they call speaking in tongues" is what God wants spoken at that particular time. Hmmm, or is it to impress others that he/she is filled with the Holy Spirit—could be misleading themselves and the assembly? Will the Holy Spirit speak through people? The answer is YES, but not to show off.

The Holy Spirit is the Power that Jesus left Christians to continue His work in this Second Earth Age (Dispensation of Time). I Corinthians 14:18 (KJV) says "I thank my God, I speak with tongues more than ye all:" That scripture like many is taken out of context, because the Apostle Paul is saying that he speaks in more foreign languages than they all, for he could speak Roman, Greek, Arabic, Chaldean plus his natural language Hebrew tongue at any given time without an interpreter so he wished that we all could. The Holy Spirit first speaks through man collectively. Read Acts 2:1-6 (KJV), when the "Day of Pentecost" had fully come was the first time the Holy Spirit spoke through men collectively. The "other tongues" (#1100 - naturally unacquired language) that was spoken on that day by them that were in the house as the Holy Spirit gave them utterance was done even in the dialect of those who were listening. Where: All the languages that were spoken are in verses Acts 2: 9-11 (KJV), so there is nothing unknown about these tongues (languages) that were spoken. The Pentecost Tongue - Cloven Tongue is best described as if you were speaking at the United Nations and everyone could understand you in their own language without the need for an interpreter, that would be the evidence of the Holy Spirit, and no man can fake that.

Question: What is the gift of tongues in the Bible?

It was and still is God's Holy Spirit that controls the tongue to speak in a language that had never been learned by the person doing the speaking. This happens in accordance to the guidance of the Holy Spirit to deliver a message from God; therefore, it's an unknown tongue to the speaker and he/she more than likely do not know what was said. Acts 2:5-8, 11 (KJV). The word "tongue" means "language" and the "gift of tongues" was and is not the ability to speak in a string of "gibberish" or "babbling;" There is nothing supernatural about that and it profits nobody and can easily be faked or simply learned. How many times do we see the "gift of tongues" exercised in God's Word? There are only three instances in the entire Word of God where the gift of tongues is exercised, and they are in Acts 2,10, and, 19 (KJV). Except for the book of I Corinthians (KJV), the gift of tongues is never referred to in any other Epistles of Paul.

Question: What was the purpose of the gift of tongues?

God sheds great light on the purpose of the gift of tongues in I Corinthians 14:22 (KJV). It clearly says, "Wherefore tongues are for a sign, not to them that believe, but to them that believe not:" One thing is clear. The gift of tongues was a sign too and for unbelievers. In context verse 22 it's obvious that Paul had unbelieving Israelites in mind. When we cross reference it with I Corinthians 1:22 (KJV), we find that the Jews require a Sign! The nation of Israel was born using miraculous Exodus 4:30-31 (KJV). Because of their stubbornness and unbelief, God has always dealt with Israel using miraculous signs. Psalm 74:9 (KJV) In the Old Testament, "strange tongues were a sign to Israel of impending judgment." (Isaiah 28:11-12 KJV; Jeremiah 5:15 KJV; Deuteronomy 28: 15-68 KJV). The Bible is clear, tongues are for a sign, the Jews required a sign and to put it simply, the "Gift of Tongues" was a sign to Israel in the book of Acts and this may explain why we never see "tongues" spoken unless there were Jews present. The gift was never given as a means of personal edification heavenly prayer language as some call it and I would like to know where that is stated in the Bible. It was a gift used to get God's truth out and to be a sign to Israel. Tongues are never spoken - or even mentioned - outside of the Acts period, because Israel's program was set aside in Acts 28: 26-28 (KJV) and I Corinthians (KJV) was written during the book of Acts.

Question: How does the story of Peter and Cornelius fit in with all of this teaching about tongues?

When the apostles were filled with the Spirit in Acts 2 (KJV); this was First Time & Witness of the Holy Spirit speaking through them at once in cloven tongues-meaning it went out in all the languages of the people who were present Acts 2:4-8 (KJV). This was a miraculous sign to Israel that authenticated the apostles' message and the fact that they were filled with God's Spirit.

Second Time & Witness

When Cornelius and his entire house of Gentiles believed Peter's message, God at once gave those Gentiles the Holy Spirit. But how would Peter know this? God gave these Gentiles the same gift that He gave to Peter and the twelve on the "Day of Pentecost" the gift of tongues Cornelius being a Roman leader of soldiers, he would have known Latin, and maybe some Greek in which Peter and the other Jews would recognize it, so it may have been Aramaic or Hebrew that they spoke, who knows for it is not said, but one thing for sure it was a language that was not of their natural tongue. This was the outward, visible, miraculous sign to Peter and the other Jews with Peter that these Gentiles had, in fact, truly received God's Spirit as those on the "Day of Pentecost" and there was no denying it Acts 10:44-46 (KJV).

When Peter had to give an account to his Jewish brethren at Jerusalem, it was the sign gift of tongues that kept Peter out of hot water Acts 11:15-18 (KJV). There are those who would like to take this story and try to make it the standard for every person that gets saved and Filled/Baptized with the Holy Spirit; but this is quite ludicrous because God is the one who chooses which Gift is given to a person who believes In and On His Son Jesus Christ by Faith. Therefore, who in these days are the Tester (s) & Witness (es) of a True Pure Language being spoken that was not learned? This was a unique, one-of-a-kind event. These Gentiles spoke in tongues that prove outwardly to Peter and all the Jews who believed and did not believe that God had, in fact, given His Holy Spirit to these Gentiles by faith alone. This was a groundbreaking event that would require a miraculous sign to convince the Jews of its validity. This event would be crucial for the future of the church and for Paul's ministry to the Gentiles. At the Jerusalem Council, it was this event that Peter would refer to in proving that the Gentiles do not have to keep the Jewish law to be saved, and that Gentiles should be included in the church by grace through faith alone Acts 15:7-11 (KJV).

Third Time & Witness

The Cloven Tongues in Acts 19:1-7 (KJV) says "And it came to pass, that, while Apollos was at Corinth, Paul having passed through the upper coasts came to Ephesus: and finding certain disciples, ² He said unto them, Have ye received the Holy Ghost since ye believed? And they said unto him, We have not so much as heard whether there be any Holy Ghost. ³ And he said unto them, Unto what then were ye baptized? And they said, Unto John's baptism. ⁴ Then said Paul, John verily baptized with the baptism of repentance, saying unto the people, that they should believe on him which should come after him, that is, on Christ Jesus. ⁵ When they heard this, they were baptized in the name of the Lord Jesus. ⁶ And when Paul had laid his hands upon them, the Holy Ghost came on them; and they spake with tongues and prophesied. ⁷ And all the men were about twelve."

Facts

The Holy Spirit will speak that Cloven Tongue again, it was done as a sign to the unbelievers in those days, as well for the gainsayers that will be here when the Elect Men and Women are delivered up before the Synagogue of Satan of them who wish to persecute them in that Hour of Temptation read Mark 13: 9 -11 (KJV), Luke 21:12 -15 (KJV), I Corinthians 14: 22 (KJV), and Revelation 17:12 (KJV).

In addition, I also will add that the Holy Spirit will speak through mankind when it is necessary for a message to be delivered to one who does not understand or speak your natural language. This can happen in two ways: one is that the (hearer/receiver) hears the words being spoken in their own language as the person who is doing the speaking is speaking in their own language and two, just as it happen on the "Day of Pentecost" the person that is speaking the *unknown* language that was not taught to him or her is by the Power of the Holy Spirit. The main thing I am trying to get across is that it's the Holy Spirit that does the speaking not the person himself/ herself. There are some Christians who believe that when the Pastor says, pray in the spirit, the Pastor is saying speak in tongues, so for those Christians who believe they have the "gift of tongue" automatically start speaking what they believe to be speaking in tongues and the humorous thing about it is that only God can understand it - I suppose or shakes His head in discuss at the confusion that is happening and the confuse man/woman who is speaking. That perception Pastor is saying speak in tongues is wrong, so what is the "Gift of Tongue" for? People please read the scriptures!

Yes, there is a guarantee time that the Holy Spirit will speak Cloven Tongues again as He did in Acts 2 (KJV), Jesus tells us when it will happen in Matthew 10: 16-20 (KJV) "Behold, I send you forth as sheep in the midst of wolves: be ye therefor wise as serpents, and harmless as doves. [17] But beware of men: for they will deliver you up to the councils, and they will scourge you in their synagogues; [18] And ye shall be brought before governors and kings for my sake, for a testimony against them and the Gentiles. [19]But when they deliver you up, take no thought how or what ye shall speak: for it shall be given you in that same hour what ye shall speak. [20] For it is not ye that speak, but the Spirit of your Father which speaketh in you."

Note

If you are one of God's Elect and you refuse to let the Holy Spirt to speak through you when delivered up before Satan and his Elect Angles, this sin is the only sin that is Unforgivable.

Again, Jesus states in Matthew12:31-32 (KJV) "Wherefore I say unto you, All manner of sin and blasphemy shall be forgiven unto men: but the blasphemy against the Holy Ghost shall not be forgiven unto men. [32] And whosoever speaketh a word against the Son of man, it shall be forgiven him: but whosoever speaketh against the Holy Ghost, it shall not be forgiven him, neither in this world, neither in the world to come." I know you may question my reasoning because Jesus said blasphemy and I say "does not allow" is the same.

The word blasphemeo is from a compound word blásphemos (New Testament (NT): 989) and blásphemos means, to be abusive and revile another's good name. The word blásphemos is a compound of two root words, blapto, (NT: 984) and pheme (NT: 5345). Blapto is a primary verb meaning, to hinder, i.e. to injure. Pheme (pronounced "fame") is from a root word phemi (NT: 5346) and means, a saying, i.e. rumor, and phemi originates from phos (NT: 5457) and phaino (NT: 5316), which means, to reveal or make one's thoughts known thru speech. Combining all the literal meanings of all the words that make up the Greek blasphemeo, a precise definition of the word translated as blasphemy in the (NT).

Think what you must, but don't let us fallout over this; put it on the shelf and come back after praying about it and keep opening the Word of God!

<u>Fifth Norm</u>: The Rapture Hmmm!

I Thessalonians 4:13-17 (KJV) and II Thessalonians 2:1-12 (KJV)

The etymology of the word "Rapture" is derived from Middle French rapture, via the Medieval Latin raptura ("seizure, kidnapping"), which derives from the Latin raptus "a carrying off.". The Koine Greek of I Thessalonians 4:17 KJV) uses the verb form ἁρπαγησόμεθα (harpagisometha), which means "we shall be caught up" or "taken away," with the connotation that this is a sudden event. The dictionary form of this Greek verb is harpazō (ἁρπάζω). This use is also seen in such texts as Acts 8:39 9 (KJV), II Corinthians 12: 2-4 (KJV), and Revelation 12:5 (KJV). The Latin Vulgate translates the Greek ἁρπαγησόμεθα as rapiemur, from the verb rapio meaning to catch up or take away.

Note

The King James Bible was not interpreted from Latin writings, but from Hebrew, Aramaic, Chaldee, and Greek Languages. The Rapture doctrine did not exist before John Darby along with some other so call preachers invented it in 1830 AD; and before it "popped into their head's no one had ever heard of a secret rapture doctrine). The word Rapture is not in the Bible, but it is a popular term used to describe one perceived view of the return of Jesus based on the writings of the I Thessalonians 4:17 (KJV) "Then we which are alive and remain shall be caught up together with them in the clouds, to meet the Lord in the air: and so shall we ever be with the Lord."

Before going further, I must break down some words into their original language so you can get a clear understanding of what the Apostle Paul was really saying. In addition, you must read before verse 17 to get the Subject of this part of the letter. One must understand that Apostle Paul spoke slang Greek and I will give you an example from one of his writing's especially about how he used the word "cloud." First word to set straight in your mind is "Air" used in verse 17: from "Strong's Exhausted Concordance" "Air:" I Thessalonians 4:17 (KJV) Greek #109 aer (ah-ayr'); from aemi (to breathe unconsciously, i.e. respire; by anal. to blow); Compare #5594 Greek word psucho: meaning to blow, to make cool. In a nut shell this "Air" that Apostle Paul is writing about is not the "Atmosphere or Sky;" but it is when God breathe or blew into all living creatures nostrils the "Breath of Life," but this time all living creatures will change from their "flesh" body into their "spiritual" body in a "twinkle of an eye." The reason being is because the Seventh Trumpet would have blown for the preparation of the return of Jesus Christ (Second Advent). Hmmm, if you cannot handle that, then put it on the shelf and now let me give you that example of Apostle Paul's slang for cloud. Hebrew 12:1 (KJV) says "Wherefore seeing we also are compassed about with so great a cloud of witnesses," this is a large gathering of people.

When Jesus Christ returns every living thing that has breath will become a spiritual being and every knee shall bawl at His coming, and those who believe "In and On" Jesus will gather together in a large crowd. This happens because they had withstood Satan's tactics and their Faith in God that He would be Faithful by His Word for Salvation of them that Believed. Now let's go to the subject and get the entire text in which Apostle Paul was writing to the Thessalonians about. The subject starts in I Thessalonians 4: 13-16 (KJV) that says "But I would not have you to be ignorant, brethren, concerning them which are asleep, that ye sorrow not, even as others which have no hope.[14] For if we believe that Jesus died and rose again, even so them also which sleep in Jesus will God bring with him. [15] For this we say unto you by the word of Lord, that we which are alive and remain unto the coming of the Lord shall not prevent them which are asleep.[16] For the Lord Himself shall descend from heaven with a shout, with the voice of the archangel, and with the trump of God: and the dead in Christ shall rise first:"

Note

That is a bad interpretation of what was written because the dead in Christ has already risen. Remember verse 14, therefore verse 16d is a contradiction of the Word, God forbid). I believe it to be the ideal spiritual condition of believers in regard to sin, if not, it has contradicted verse14. Pray!

II Thessalonians 2: 1-12 (KJV) says "Now we beseech you, brethren, by the coming of our Lord Jesus Christ, and by our gathering together unto him, ²That ye be not soon shaken in mind, or be troubled, neither by spirit, nor by word, nor by letter as from us, as that the day of Christ is at hand.³ Let no man deceive you by any means: for that day shall not come, except there come a falling away first, and that man of sin be revealed, the son of perdition;" ⁴ Who opposeth and exalteth himself above all that is called God, or that is worshiped; so that he as God sitteth in the temple of God, shewing himself that he is God. ⁵ Remember ye not, that, when I was yet with you, I told you these things? ⁶ And now ye know what withholdeth that he might be revealed in his time. ⁷ For the mystery of iniquity doth already work: only he who now letteth will let, until he be taken out of the way. ⁸ And then shall that Wicked be revealed, whom the Lord shall consume with the spirit of his mouth, and shall destroy with the brightness of his coming: ⁹ Even him, whose coming is after the working of Satan with all power and signs and lying wonders, ¹⁰And with all deceivableness of unrighteousness in them that perish; because they received not the love of the truth, that they might be saved. ¹¹ And for this cause God shall send them strong delusion, that they should believe a lie: ¹² That they all might be damned who believed not the truth, but had pleasure in righteousness."

Notes

No other than Satan himself, because he is the only one named to perish that means perdition. Remember what God said in Ezekiel 28:18c (KJV) "therefore will I bring forth a fire from the midst of thee, it shall devour thee, and I will bring thee to ashes upon the earth in the sight of all them that behold thee."

God is speaking about Christians who want to hang onto "Traditions of Men," and God gave Ezekiel His Word that has come to pass in our generation today especially when using different translations to teach the people to believe a lie.

Ezekiel 13: 1-7 (KJV) says "And the word of the LORD came unto me, saying, ² Son of man, prophesy say thou unto them that prophesy out of their own hearts, Hear ye the word of the LORD; ³ Thus saith the Lord GOD; Woe unto the foolish prophets, that follow their own spirit, and have seen nothing! ⁴ O Israel, thy prophets are like the foxes in the deserts. ⁵ Ye have not gone up into the gaps, neither made up the hedge for the house of Israel to stand in the battle in the day of the LORD. ⁶ They have seen vanity and lying divination, saying, The LORD saith: and the LORD hath not sent them: and they have made others to hope that they would confirm the word. ⁷ Have ye not seen a vain vision, and have ye not spoken a lying divination, whereas ye say, The LORD saith it; albeit I have not spoken?"

Note

Remember I told you that John Darby along with some other preachers invented the Rapture Theory in 1830 AD. These preachers had stolen this theory from a Scottish woman named Margaret MacDonald who had a so call vision from God about the Pretribulation, and the preachers called it "Rapture" when they was finish with it. It was easier for them to teach and preach it for everyone to accept this lie, because it was from a woman and in those days no one would believe a woman because it was and still is taught in some churches that women are not to teach or preach God's Word.

Here is what God had said about that lie

Ezekiel 13: 17-23 (KJV) says "Likewise, thou son of man, set thy face against the daughters of thy people, which prophesy out of their own heart; and prophesy thou against them, ¹⁸ And say, Thus saith the Lord GOD; Woe to the women that sew pillows to all armholes and make kerchiefs upon the head of every stature to hunt souls! Will ye hunt the souls of my people, and will ye save the souls alive that come unto you? ¹⁹ And will ye pollute me among my people for handfuls of barley and for pieces of bread, to slay the souls that should not die, and to save the souls alive that should not live, by your lying to my people that hear your lies? ²⁰ Wherefore thus saith the Lord GOD; Behold, I am against your pillows, wherewith ye there hunt the souls to make them fly, and I will tear them from your arms, and will let the souls go, even the souls that ye hunt to make them fly. ²¹ Your kerchiefs also will I tear, and deliver my people out of your hand, and they shall be no more in your hand to be hunted; and ye shall know that I am the LORD. ²² Because with lies ye have made the heart of the righteous sad, whom I have not made sad; and strengthened the hands of the wicked, that he should not return from his wicked way, by promising him life: ²³ Therefore ye shall see no more vanity, nor divine divinations: for I will deliver my people out of your hand: and ye shall know that I am the LORD."

Do not get it twisted, most educated preachers will preach Ezekiel 13:17-23 from the NIV Bible translation and when you get to verse twenty, it says something about Birds. Now I wonder who came up with that, could it have been the Kenites (sons of Cain) that I spoke about and they were scribes for the Tribe of Judah (King Line) in I Chronicles 2:55 (KJV)?

Note

When you see LORD, it is referring to God's sacred name YHVA that is in the Book of Esther.

I have given you a lot of meat between the two slices of bread of the sandwich I want you to eat, just remember there is no Rapture – flying away because God has equipped His Saints with the Word, and all the Armour they will need to defeat their enemies. I did not see any Jetpack in that list of Armour in Ephesians 6: 10-18 (KJV). But thank God in the name of Jesus Christ (Yeshua) meaning God's Savior we who believe gave us Power over "All" our enemies, and if we "Endure until the End" we shall be saved and inherit "Eternal life." Therefore, stay in constant Prayer, guard Your Ear Gates and Eye Gates; my suggestion is when necessary go to your Prayer Closet or Quit Place and let the Holy Spirit "Spiritually Circumcise Your Heart and Mind!"

Just a Reminder

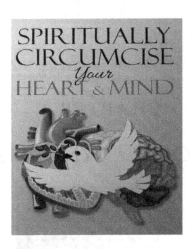

All Souls belong to GOD, and every person has Free Will
to Choose to LOVE God or Follow SATAN? It is Your
Salvation and you can sail your ship anyway you want too,
but to receive The Power what Jesus has already given us
to be Overcomers; Repent and Learn how to use it because
Jesus paid an Awesome Price for Our Sins. Therefore,
Spiritually Circumcise Your Heart and Mind Now!

A Christian's True Purpose Will Be Fulfilled When God's Holy
Spirit Continuously Flows from their Heart to their Mind!

CHAPTER 2

BOOK 2 SYNOPSIS

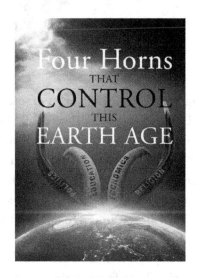

This book was written from a Perspective and Prospective view within the Spiritual and Practical realm of Life during this World/Earth Age (Dispensation of Time) we are living in; and a book of how this World (Town, City, County, State or Country) is operated on a daily basis. Throughout the book I used the "Four Horns" from a cogitation prospective of Positive–"Power of Truth" and Negative–"Power of Falsity" to get my point across as how effective they are used. In addition, of how and why they have come about and against a set of people to belittle them, especially People of Color. I like to use the Spiritual side of the Four Horns that are mentioned in many places in the King James Version (KJV) Bible; for they signify the Power of Truth for good and the Power of Falsity for Evil.

Note

Horns signifies Power! Examples: Genesis 22: 13 (KJV) "Then Abraham raised his eyes and looked, and behold, behind him a ram caught in the thicket by his horns; and Abraham went and took the ram and offered him up for a burnt offering in the place of his son." Exodus 27:2 (KJV) says "You shall make its horns on its four corners; its horns shall be of one piece with it, and you shall overlay it with bronze." Psalm 75:10 (KJV) says "And all the horns of the wicked He will cut off, But the horns of the righteous will be lifted up." Zechariah 1:18 (KJV) says "Then I lifted up my eyes and looked, and behold, there were four horns."

I started using the Spiritual aspect of the Four Horns because I believe before anything is manifest itself in this physically realm of life, it starts in the spiritual realm in which we cannot see, but where we all came from with a divine purpose. I like to use the Prayer that Jesus taught His Disciples after they asked Him how to pray.

Note

Majority of Christians calls this the Lord's Prayer, but it's not; this is what Jesus taught His disciples how to pray after they asked him. Matthew 6:9-13 (KJV) says [9] "In this manner, therefore, pray: Our Father in heaven, Hallowed be Your name. [10]Your kingdom come. Your will be done On earth as it is in heaven. [11] Give us this day our daily bread. [12]And forgive us our debts, As we forgive our debtors. [13]And do not lead us into temptation, But deliver us from the evil one. For yours is the kingdom and the power and the glory forever. Amen."

Noticed that Jesus begins the Prayer with whom everything starts with, The Father-God who is in Heaven (Spiritual Realm) then it will manifest into the World (Physical Realm) of life if it be the Will of God. The actual Prayer of Jesus is in Matthew 26: 39 & 42 (KJV) says [39b] "O my Father, if it be possible, let this cup pass from me: nevertheless, not as I will, but as thou wilt. [42b] "O my Father, if this cup may not pass away from me, except I drink it, thy will be done." The "Cup" Jesus is referring to is the "Wrath of God" mentioned in the Book of Revelation 16:1 (KJV) "And I heard a great voice out of the temple saying to the seven angels, Go your ways, and pour out the vials of the wrath of God upon the earth."

The ***Spirituality of the Four Horns*** *is* taken from the Bible and I use as a reference and guidance is the most significance of what I am trying to get across to you!

(1) As Prophetic Signs: I Kings 22:11 (KJV) and II Chronicles 18:10 (KJV)

(2) Describing God's Saving Power: II Samuel 22: 2-3 (KJV), Psalm 18:2 (KJV) and Luke 1:69 (KJV)

(3) Describing Human Strength: Deuteronomy 33:17 (KJV) and many other scriptures in (KJV)

(4) Symbolizing the Power of World Rulers and Enemies of God: Zechariah 1: 18-21 (KJV)

(5) Symbolizing the Power of Jesus Christ: Revelation 5:6 (KJV).

My deepest suggestion for you is to pray for God's Holy Spirit to reveal to you what is truth and if what I have put before you is truth, real and relevant. I know most people have heard that "We are living in the Last Days," but now I believe it to be even more of a truth than ever, because of the "Prophecies" being fulfilled on a daily, weekly, monthly and yearly basis.

The Practicality of the Four Horns where taken from research and a paper I wrote while attending James Madison University for my Bachelors of Individual Studies Degree, my Major was "Socioeconomics" and a Minor in "Small Business and Entrepreneurship." The foundation of my Degree was based on the Four Horns (Economics, Education, Politics and Religion). In addition, my Thesis for graduation was on the "Socioeconomics of Harrisonburg Virginia" and I used the Four Horns (Economics, Education, Politics and Religion) as its foundation. In addition, I referenced five papers

I wrote for varies Sociology class in 1999-2000 and recently updated most of them in 2015-2016 with the last paper having four sub-titles.

Practicality of the 4 Horns

(1) Synopsis of *"Behind the Official Story"* Chapter 1 of *"Domination and the Arts of Resistance Hidden Transcripts"* by James C. Scott; I wrote *"Image Is Everything!"* for Sociology 490 on December 17, 1998, and revised in 2015: Introduction – Definitions of (Economics, Education, Politics and Religion); Chapter 1 "Eurocentrism," Chapter 2 "The Inherent Battles of Most Black People," Chapter III "America what are You Going to Do?" and Summary.

Behind the Official Story a person must understand clearly what are hidden and public transcripts, what are the purposes behind them, realize how things are done in society as a whole, because of these transcripts and how it affects politics in society. Since "politics is involved in everything we do in our society," therefore I will use five W's in an example of questions and answers to express my opinions of the materials I have read, and my understandings from the lectures concerning this chapter and politics in society. The **five W's** for this chapter:

(1) <u>What</u> are hidden and public transcripts?
(2) <u>Who</u> mainly writes these transcripts and whom does it benefit?
(3) <u>When</u> are they written?
(4) <u>Where</u> are they written?
(5) <u>Why</u> are they written the way they are?

The best definition I can give you for "Hidden and Public Transcripts" are:

a.) Hidden Transcript (s): They are either written or silent, but they mostly resist against whatever public transcript (s) it may go against.
b.) Public Transcript (s): Transcript (s) that are made available for the public and some are official, and some are unofficial.
Example: "Official Transcripts" are written laws, and "Unofficial Transcripts" are newspapers.

Note

I believe this quote from George Eliot "there is no action possible without a little acting;" because most actions come from feelings, beliefs, surroundings, observations, and what has been taught. We learn how to act in given situations of life, and then the performance is given. When Power is seen in social forms the people of different status act according to that "Power" or "Authority" that confronts them.

James C. Scott begins this chapter talking about Power, how the recognition of "Power" is seen in a social form, and what is required from people of different status to act according to that Power or Authority that confronts them. Then he talks about Public Transcripts and Hidden Transcripts, and how these Transcripts form the actions of people of different status.

A person who is rich automatically gains some type of Power, because their money has great influences in this society, and along with that, they are expected to act and carry themselves a certain way; so now the act or performance has to begin. Once this person or group of people are set up in this status of being rich or belonging to the Elite's, then they are given authority to act according to the amount of money they have. Most public transcripts that run our country have multiple hidden transcripts within the public transcript if you look very hard to get a close understanding of what the public transcript really means. Power and Authority go together, and those who have power, their authority is to enforce or make sure the enforcement of public transcripts are carried out for society to govern themselves accordingly. The person that does not have this type of power is classified as subordinates. Being a subordinate is occupying a lower class, rank, or position, but in this chapter, I understand it as inferior to and controlled by those who have authority and power in this society. I do not like the word inferior, because it is taken so much out of context. Inferior has the same meaning as subordinate to a point, but in a more demeaning way.

(I)   What are public and hidden transcripts? James C. Scott uses the term public transcript "as a shorthand way of describing the open interaction between subordinates and those who dominate." To make it simple, public transcripts are transcripts that are made available for the public, and some are for the public to govern themselves according to what is written. For example, the law that is written. You have some public transcripts that are against one another, and some that are silent, but most important is the validity within it. The validity will describe if it is contradictory, supplementary, or complementary; not saying that one cannot have all three within the contents of its writing, but one must look very hard at what they read for clarity of understanding.

Hidden Transcripts can be either written or silent, but are not so much of content, but they mostly resist against whatever public transcripts it may go against. James C. Scott said "many, perhaps most, hidden transcripts remain just that: hidden from the public view and never enacted." Depending on the hidden transcript, some can be secret documents that are hidden from the public until they are discovered by others than who they were written or meant for, and then it becomes a public transcript. Another example is that there are no written hidden transcripts, which can be in songs, type of language being used, pictures, signs/signals that are given, or doing the opposite of what has been written or said in the face or behind closed doors from the authority of the public transcripts.

A good example in this chapter of the book of both public and hidden transcripts is between Squire Donnithorne imposing on Mr. and Mrs. Poyser. On all those occasions prior to Mrs. Poyser objection in public, she managed to keep up the pretense of being deferential and agreeable, which made it a Dominate and Subordinate public transcript. But once she could not hold it within herself, the hidden transcript came out as a reactionary effect that triggered her most inner thoughts about the situation at hand. James C. Scott said "each participant will be familiar with the public transcripts and the hidden transcript of his or her circle, but not with the hidden transcript of the other. For this reason, political analysis can be advanced by research that can compare the hidden transcript of subordinate groups with the hidden transcript of the powerful and both hidden transcripts with the public transcript they share."

I believe you cannot have one without the other, because there is always some type of resistance, it be positive or negative. The big question is, who is the "Dominate" and who is the "Subordinate" to the public transcript that needs to be followed at that given time or situation? We have many types of public transcripts, and the one I want to give an example of is in the form of a picture, because it is said "a picture is worth a thousand words." The words that are silent means a lot to those people or groups of people whom the picture is intended for. It can be positive to one, and negative to the other, that's the way public transcripts work in general, because they will never satisfy everyone. The picture I am talking about most of is the pictures of Jesus Christ. Most Christians in the United States, if not the world, think Jesus Christ was a white man just because most photographs portrayed Him as a "white man" who had blond hair, and blue eyes. Now I will comment on the remaining four W's in the form of questions and answers.

(II)   Why are most photographs of Jesus Christ portray him being a white man? My answer: the elite, powerful and mostly rich people in America are white, so it would only be right if the person everyone says came to save the world from their sins and died on the cross for them and resurrected into the heavens was a white man. The hidden transcript behind this is for white people to believe that they are above all the others in this world, and everyone of color is inferior to them.

(III)   Who made it like that and for what reason? My answer: Satan through the Kenites and "Elite's" mainly in the religious orders are the cause of this strife, because where there's strife there's no unity or love. God is "Love" and as long as Satan can work can keep people from loving one another then the further they will be from the "Truth" and God, and that's his main purpose.

(IV)   When and Where does this picture be seen? Most people would say it's just a picture, but I say it's more than that. Everyone knows that 11 a.m. to about 1 p.m. on Sundays is the most segregated hours in the United States; because it is church time for the majority of the churches, but regardless of the time most churches have some type of picture of

32

Jesus Christ in it and it portrays him as a white man. Another example: when the Pope visits certain countries, there is a giant photograph of Jesus Christ white as snow used as the background for the stage. Is the Pope a White man? Not, but their skin color is not "Brown or Black" therefore the "Elites" of the major religions in the world who believes in Jesus Christ since the time Christianity came to Europe, that's when and where I think this falsehood started from.

Hidden transcripts that counteract public transcripts deviates the performances of the dominants and subordinates in public. The rich and powerful are to govern themselves in one way, and the subordinate in another way, this is what is expected of them just because who they are. Along with the act and performance is the mask. Each group has a mask that they wear, and without the mask there is no great performance. We discussed masking, and this mask is not talking about a mask you buy; but the one you wear on the inside as well as the outside, with this a person or group of people can get their point across or try to make a good impression of themselves.

When performing a public or Hidden Transcript one uses his/her mask to only satisfy the requirements of the transcript. Their actions and expectations of them while in a circumstance they are in could be life threatening or removal from a position of authority by the ones who put them in that position because they did not fit in. Masking is a form of a hidden transcript that one must master for themselves, and in some cases this mask is worn corporately.

Validity of speech and validity of written words play an important role, because how one speaks and writes may mean one thing to one group of people, and another meaning to the ones who they are really meant for within the Transcript. For this reason, we have Hidden Transcripts within a Public Transcript, because it's not written for all people to understand or obey, but mostly for the subordinate people to follow. For example, the language that's used it writing books for lawyers and doctors, they fully understand what's written and the meaning behind the contents, but the average person has to ask them what it said; and you always can't believe what you hear. This validity works in both directions, Hidden Transcripts can be in the form of songs, well the validity of that song has many meanings, but to some it's an import meaning that will cause action and that's to the one it's being sung too. I think there's only one true Public Transcript, and everything that man has come up with has been forms of Hidden Transcripts. The Hidden Transcripts are brought to the forefront through the power of Satan by way of the Kenites and Elites of this world to take the place of the living Word of God.

(1) "How Europe Underdeveloped Africa" & "How Capitalism Underdeveloped Black America" (Paper written by Timothy L. Walker for Sociology 102 Summer Course1996)

Before getting to the two question at hand, I first want to introduce a little history about the European cultural, thought, and behavior I arrived from reading some abstracts of "Yurugu An African-centered Critique of European Cultural Thought and Behavior" by Marimba Ani (Dona Richards). Throughout your reading refer to some key things that are brought out by Yurugu, I think a person should know who the people are before asking "How."

Yurugu expressed the character of European Utamawazo was that the impression people have is that Platonic thoughts ushered in vast and immediate changes for European culture. In a sense, no "Europe" in his time, but in another sense, European Asili had already been planted as the seed of culture. This seed had taken place in the early days of Indo-European tribal development, where there were already definite uamaroho, or even earlier with the first homosapiens that inhabit the Eurasian Steppes and the Caucasus region for a long period to become non-African.

Plato's work was even more important in the definitional process of the utamawazo, because it had been prefigured in the germ of the culture, necessary if the Asili was to be realized. European history is a history of bloody internecine wars heretics, infidel, barbarians, and battles fought to keep a particular character to eliminate opposing influences: It is a history of aggressive behavior towards other cultures. All differences threaten the realization of the Asili, and it was like a child struggle to be born.

The battle is fought because the Asili exist, and the Platonic thought is a significant determinative, because it is suited for the Asili. His epistemological theory helped in the formulation of an utamawazo that complemented the Asili. With Plato, epistemology became the ideological, and contrary to what some have claimed; Platonic conceptions did not make knowledge accessible to the masses through its desacralization. What he did was to ensure that at least until the "Gutenberg Galaxy;" the few would have no threat from the many, because the many did not have access to the intellectual life of the State.

This was due to a lot of factors, but most important was that only the privileged few were trained to be literate in this sense. Plato's plan was foolproof; because even when the European masses gained access centuries later, the mechanisms of control were so tightly structured that the assumptions they had to assimilate to be considered educated guaranteed that they would think the way he planned. It was as though his hand reached through centuries of cultural existence, as the European cognitive style and utamawazo became an extension of Platonism.

It came to pass that not only did all European intellectuals would be trained in the academy (Plato's legacy), but all intellectuals, for this testament became the success of European cultural imperialism. The academy had preserved a cultural tradition, a race of people, and a dominant society. No matter the internecine controversies and so-called political revolutions that might occur, the Academy ensured that the ideological infrastructure would remain intact. The emergent theme of power!

The European objective to Power was not that of Power-to-Do, but Power-Over. Power-to-Do seeks balance and harmony, whereby Power-over functions only through the modality of control. It precludes cosmic, communal, and or sympathetic relationship. It is political and materialistic.

The Asili seed of culture prefigures, then dictates, the development of structures, institutions, and arrangements that will facilitate the achievement of power-over-others. The forms that are created within the European cultural experience can then be understood as mechanisms of control in the pursuit of power. That is what they all have in common, and that is the key to their cultural explanation. The ideological base of the cultural is the will-to-power, and the utamawazo or culturally structured thought reorders the universe into relationships that prepares it for the illusion of control. Separation comes first, then the Asili forces its own self-realization through the cognitive structure of the utamawazo in the following manner:

Dichotomization: All realities are split into two parts. Self-split from Other. The process continues until the universe is composed of disparate entities.

Oppositional, Confrontational, Antagonistic Relationships: The Self knows itself, because it is placed in opposition to Other that includes the natural and affective part of the Self. This self-awareness is the origin of European consciousness; the Other which is perceived to be different from the self-is-threatening, therefore establishing an antagonistic relationship between all entities that are different.

Note

This presents a principle of confrontational relationships in all realities; indeed, cognition itself is made possible through confrontation.

Hierarchical Segmentation: The original splitting and separating mental process assigns qualitatively different unequal value to the opposing realities of the dichotomies, and a stratification of value to all realities within a given set of categories. The effect is to cut the possibility of organic or sympathetic relationship, thereby, setting up grounds for the dominance of the superior form or phenomenon over that is perceived to be inferior. Power-relationship!

Analytical, Nonsynthetic Thought: Realities are torn apart in order to be known. Culturally this tendency inhibits the movement to a higher, more synthesizing level of understanding. It is on the level of synthesis that opposition would be resolved and given the fundamental premises of this cognitive system there would no longer be any basis for knowledge. Power-over-other!

Objectification: The conceptualization of pure thoughts is made possible by a cognitive emphasis on absolutism and abstractification. Self creates the proper objects of knowledge through the act of controlling that which is inferior to it in a phenomenal sense.

Absolutist-Abstractification: This also mandates the universalization as well as the reification of truths. A universalism dictated by the need to use epistemology as a power tool and as a mechanism of control.

Rationalism and Scientism: According to them (Self) would have you believe that all reality had been created by the European mind for the purpose of control. Intense rationalism is the ultimate experience of control for the European mind. Ideologically, it justifies the control of the European "self- over-others."

Scientism: Is the merger of religion and rationality. In addition, the need to experience control creates a scientistic Utamawazo in which predictability and rationality helped to defend the knowing Self against any possible threat from the unknown. European god became the great scientist and the rationalist pursuit is the creation of moral behavior.

Authoritative Literate Mode: The Written Symbol becomes authoritative utterance, enabling the European mind to further objectify reality as it universalizes European control. More control, more power!

Desacralization: This is a necessary by-product of all the characteristics of the European Utamawazo. As nature is alienated, objectified, and approached with a quantifying mentality; this views the universe as material reality only to be acted upon by the superior mind.

The pursuit of Power is the nature of the European Asili; while the Utamawazo is one manifestation of the Asili created to assist in the realization of the Asili. These characteristics encourage the development of a technical order and imperialistic behavior towards other cultures through the underdevelopment of that culture.

Development and underdevelopment are not only comparative terms, but they also have a dialectical relationship with one another whereby, the two help produce each other by intersection. Western Europe and Africa had a relationship, it insured the transfer of wealth from Africa to Europe. This happen because trade became international, and in late fifteenth century when Africa and Europe first had a common relationship-along with Asia and the Americas. The major advantage for Europe during the fifteenth century was the internationalization of trade; owning and directing the great majority of the world's sea-going vessels and controlled the financing of trade between four continents. Africans had little clue as to the tri-continental links between Africa, Europe, and Americas. Europe had a monopoly of knowledge about the international exchange system seen, for Western Europe was the only sector capable of viewing the system as a whole.

Europeans used the superiority of their ships and cannons to gain control of all the world's waterways, starting with the western Mediterranean and the Atlantic coast of North Africa. Other countries were very much interested in the trade business in Africa; but Europe had master minded that operation of trade and assumed the Power to make decisions within the international trading system. Therefore, if anyone got in their way, they would suffer the consequences of war; because the so-called international law for the high seas was nothing more than European law. As I see it, African people and Others were simply the victims who got in the way of development for the Europeans.

The interest Europe had in Africa went deeper than captives and slaves that belonged to African kings and rulers; because it was all the riches and commodities Africa had to offer, and Europe was not going to letting it get out of their hands. Europe was intending to have it all, and by any means necessary to it; and it didn't matter who had what they wanted, they went against them to get it or they would let them take part in trade only to become a victim themselves.

To discuss trade between Africans and Europeans in the four centuries before colonial rule is virtually to discuss slave trade. Africans only became a slave when he or she reached a society where they worked as a slave. Before that, he or she was first a free person and then became captive into a slave. These captives and slaves were shipped to various other parts of the world where they were to live and work as the property of Europeans; the shipments were all by Europeans who had control of the market of slaves, and this was in the interest of European capitalism and nothing else.

During this period of European dominance of the sea, in East Africa and the Sudan; many Africans were taken and sold to Arab buyers, and this was known as the Arab Slave Trade. To say that, when Europeans shipped Africans to European buyers it was the "European Slave Trade" form Africa. The number one commodity were slaves and Africa were the breeding grounds-simply the victims. For a few exceptions, European buyers bought Africans captives on the coast of Africa and the transaction between themselves and Africans was a form of trade, but the process by which captive were obtained on African soil was not trade at all. It was through warfare, trickery, banditry, and kidnapping.

Throughout the seventeenth-and eighteenth centuries, and for most of the nineteenth century, the exploitation of Africa and African labor continued to be a source for the accumulation of capital to be reinvested in Western Europe. The African contribution to European capitalist growth extended over such vital sectors as shipping, insurance, the formation of companies, capitalist agriculture, technology, and the manufacture of machinery. The effects were so wide-ranging that many are seldom brought to the notice of the reading public. Because of Africa's riches, such as dyes, camwood, Brazil wood, cochineal, gum and ivory enriched many merchants in London's Mincing Lane; and provided the raw material for industries in England, France, Germany, Switzerland, and North America-producing items ranging from knife handles to piano keys.

I must mention it now before going on, that the Europeans initially borrowed a great deal of nautical instrumentation from the North Africans, but the North Africans made no further worthwhile advances in instrumentation due to European concern of them not doing so. Remember, I mention it before that Europeans would stop at nothing of getting what they wanted; well a good example is the British used Dutch know-how as a basis for surpassing the Dutch themselves, and by the eighteenth century the Atlantic was their laboratory. It is said, that the slave trade was a training ground for the British seamen, but more significant to note that the Atlantic trade was the stimulator of consistent advances in naval technology.

The most spectacular feature in Europe which related to African trade was the rise of seaport towns notably, Bristol, Liverpool, Nantes, Bordeaux, and Seville. Because of these ports, there often emerged manufacturing centers which gave rise to the Industrial Revolution. In England, it was the county of Lancashire which was the first center of the Industrial Revolution, and the economic advance in Lancashire depended first of all on the growth of the port of Liverpool through slave trading. The connections between slavery and capitalist in the growth of England is documented by Eric Williams in his well-known book Capitalism and Slavery.

European development became Africa's underdevelopment, because the massive loss of able-bodied young men and young women. Slave buyers preferred their victims between the ages of fifteen and thirty-five, but preferable in the early twenties; the sex ratio being about two men to one woman. When you take away a country's natural resources, labor force, and its most prominent reproductive force of human beings; then what is left of that country's prior development? Therefore, African economic activity was affected both directly and indirectly by population loss; and during the colonial period when African able-bodied men left their homes as migrant laborers upset the farming routine in the home districts that often caused famines. Slave trading after all meant migration of labor in a manner one hundred times more brutal and disruptive. Before going on, I must mention United States was involved in the European slave trade.

During this period Europeans had the dominant population; they completely transferred their capitalist institutions to North America than to any other part of the globe, whereby, establishing a powerful form of capitalism-after eliminating the indigenous inhabitants and exploiting the labor of millions of Africans. The Pan Africanist, W. E. B. Du Bois, in a study of the American slave trade, quoted a report of 1862 as follows: "The number of persons engaged in the slave trade and the amount of capital embarked in it exceed our powers of calculation. The city of New York has been until of late 1862 the principal port of the world for this infamous commerce; although the cities of Portland and Boston were only second to her in distribution." American economic development up to mid-nineteenth century rest squarely on foreign commerce, of which slavery was a pivot.

Europe kept slavery in places that were physically remote from European society; therefore, inside Europe itself capitalist relations were elaborated without being adversely affected by slavery in the Americas. However, even in Europe there came a moment when the leading capitalist states found that the trade in slaves and the use of slave labor in the Americas was no longer in the interest of their further development. Britain made this decision early in the nineteenth century, to be followed by France.

All the "European Power" was becoming aware that the activities connected with producing captives from Africa was starting to be inconsistent with other economic pursuits. Britain in particular wanted Africans to collect palm produce, rubber, and grow agricultural crops for export in place of slaves; because slave raiding was violently conflicting with that objective in Western, Eastern, and Central Africa.

The truth is that a developing Africa went into slave trading and European commercial relations as into a gale-force wind, which shipwrecked a few societies, set many others off course, and slowed down the rate of advancement. However, it must be noted that African captains were still making decisions before 1885, though already forces were at work which caused European capitalist to insist on and succeed in taking over command.

Education is undeniably one of the facets of European life which had grown most appreciably during the capitalist epoch. Through education and extensive use of the written word, Europeans were able to pass on to the others the scientific principles of the material world which they had discovered, as well as a body of varied philosophical reflections on man and society.

Africans were quick to appreciate advantages deriving from a literate education. The search for European education began before the colonial period. Coastal rulers and traders recognized the necessity to penetrate more deeply into the way of life of the white man who came across the sea. The mulatto sons of white traders and sons of African rulers were the ones who made the greatest effort to learn the white man's ways.

Europeans were also racially motivated to seek political domination over Africa. The nineteenth century was one in which white racism was most violently and openly expressed in capitalist societies; with the United States as the focal point, and Britain taking the lead among the Western European capitalist nations. Africans everywhere fought against alien political rule and had to be subdued by superior force. Although a sizable minority did insist that their trade connections with Europe should remain unbroken, because of the extent they already depended on Europe. In sub-Saharan Africa and especially in West Africa, the export of slaves declined most rapidly where Europeans were prepared to buy other commodities. As soon as inhabitants of any region found that they had a product which Europeans were accepting in place of the former slave trade, those inhabitants put tremendous effort into organizing the alternative: namely, ivory, rubber, palm products, and groundnuts.

The first four centuries of Afro-European trade in a very sense represent the root of African underdevelopment. Colonialism flourished rapidly from a European viewpoint, because several of its features were already rooted in Africa in the preceding period. One of the most decisive features of the colonial system was the presence of African serving as economic, political, and cultural agents of the European colonialist. Those agents, or compradors, were already serving European interest in the pre-colonial period. The impact of trade with Europe had reduced many African rulers to the status of middlemen for European trade; thereby, it had raised ordinary Africans to that same middleman commercial role; and it created a new trading group of mixed blood, the children of Europeans or Arab fathers. Those types can all be referred to as compradors and played a key role in extending European activity from the coast into the hinterland, as soon as Europeans thought of taking over Political Power.

One of the most striking features of the nineteenth century West African history is the way Africans returned from slavery under European masters and helped in the establishment of colonial rule. This was especially true of Africans who returned from West Indies and North America to Sierra Leone or who were released from slave ships and landed in Sierra Leone, and it also applied to Africans who were once in Brazil. African agents were recruited by Europeans during colonial rule in Africa to serve in the armies that conquered Africa in the bloody period from the 1880s through the First World War started by Europeans in 1914. It is a widespread characteristic of colonialism to find agents of repression from among the colonial victims themselves.

It is true that many Africans who had little or nothing to do with pre-colonial trade also allied themselves with European newcomers. The gap in levels of political organization between Europe and Africa was very crucial. The development of political unity in form of large states was continuing steadily in Africa at the time of the Berlin Conference, Africa was still a continent of numerous socio-political groupings who had not arrived at a common purpose. Therefore, it was easy for the European intruder to play the classic game of divide and conquer. Many African rulers sought a European alliance to deal with their own African neighbor, with whom they were in conflict with. Few of those African rulers appreciated the implication of their actions, and they did not think the Europeans had come to stay permanently and to conquer not some but all Africans.

This partial and inadequate view of the world was itself a testimony of African underdevelopment relative to Europe, which in the nineteenth century was self-confidently seeking dominion in every part of the globe.

It is widely accepted that Africa was colonized because of its weaknesses. The concept of weakness should be understood as military weakness, inadequate economic capacity, and certain political weakness; namely, the incompleteness of the establishment of nation-states, which left the continent divided, and the low level of consciousness concerning the world at large, which had already been transformed into a single system by the expansion of capitalist relations.

Colonial Africa fell within the part of the international capitalist economy from which surplus was drawn to feed the metropolitan sector. Exploitation of land and labor is essential for human social advance, but only on the assumption that the product is made available within the area where exploitation takes place. Colonialism was not merely a system of exploitation, but one whose essential purpose was to repatriate the profits to the so-called mother country. That amounted to consistent expatriation of surplus produced by African resources and meant the development of Europe as part of the same dialectical process in which Africa was underdeveloped.

By any standards, labor was cheap in Africa, and the amount of surplus extracted from the African laborer was great; whereby the wages were extremely low and insufficient to keep the worker physically alive, therefore he had to grow food to survive. This applied to farm labor of plantation type, to work in mines, and certain forms of urban employment. At the time of the imposition of European colonial rule, Africans were able to gain a livelihood from the land. Many kept some contact with the land in the years ahead, and they worked away from their shambas in order to pay taxes or because they were forced to do so. After feudalism in Europe had ended, the worker had absolutely no means of sustenance other than through the sale of his labor to capitalist.

European capitalist in Africa had added racial justifications for dealing unjustly with African workers. The racist theory that the black man was inferior led to the conclusion that he deserved lower wages; and, the light-skinned Arab and Berber populations of North Africa were treated as blacks by the white racist French. Colonial governments discriminated against the employment of Africans in senior categories; and, whenever it happens that a white and black filled the same post, the white man was sure to be paid considerably more. This was true at all levels, but Africans salaried workers in the British colonies of Gold Coast and Nigeria were better off than their brothers in many other parts of the continent but were restricted to the "junior staff" level in the civil service.

For an example, European civil servants in the Gold Coast received an average of 40 pounds per month and Africans got an average of 4 pounds. That's a 10 to 1 ratio, and no one can develop themselves or survive individually off of that. In one instance where one European in an establishment earned as much as his twenty-five African assistants put together. Outside civil service, Africans obtained work in building projects, mines, and domestics, all low-paying jobs. In all colonial territories' wages were reduced during the period of crisis which shook the capitalist world during the 1930s, and they were not restored or increased until after the last capitalist world war.

In the background of the colonial scene hovered the banks, insurance companies, maritime underwriters, and other financial houses. The peasant was in the background; because they never dealt directly with such institutions, and was ignorant of their exploiting functions, therefore, the peasant or worker had no access to bank loans because he had no securities or collateral. Banks and finance houses dealt only with other capitalist who could prove to the bankers that whatever happened the bank would recover its money and make a profit. In the epoch of imperialism, the bankers became the aristocrats of the capitalist world; therefore, they were very much in the foreground. The amount of surplus produced by Africans workers and peasants that passed into the hands of metropolitan bankers was quite phenomenal; and they registered a return on capital higher than the mining companies, because each new direct investment spilled further alienation of the fruits of African labor.

The principal functions of the colonial government were to protect national interest against competition from other capitalists, to arbitrate the conflicts between their own capitalists, and to guarantee optimum conditions under which private companies could exploit Africans. The last one mention is the most crucial, because that is why colonial government were repeatedly about the maintenance of law and order; they really meant the maintenance of conditions most favorable to the expansion of capitalist and the plunder of Africa. This led to the colonial government to impose taxes, but the tax money that was collected was never put back into the colonies.

To fully understand the colonial period, it is necessary to think in terms of economic partition of Africa. At least twenty-five percent of the labor force died annually from starvation and disease, the worst period was from 1922 to 1929. Colonialism strengthened the Western European ruling class and capitalism particularly in later phases, because it was giving a new lease on life to a mode of production that was otherwise dying. From every viewpoint other than that of the minority class of capitalists, because colonialism was monstrously holding back the liberation of mankind. Remember throughout that time of European control, the United States got a bigger slice of the unequal trade balance between the metropoles and colonial Africa.

All these things led to *"How Capitalism Underdeveloped Black America."* Remember from the beginning most of the people in America were Europeans, and the capitalist system in America was at its highest level. Black people in the United States were the direct product of massive economic and social forces during that historical juncture; therefore, it created the early capitalist overseas production of rice, sugar, and cotton for consumption by Europe's western core. That labor power of Afro-American slaves drove world accumulation that helped European modern capitalism. In the proverbial bowels of the capitalist leviathan, the slaves forged a new world culture with its origins in Africa, and in its creative forms was something entirely new. The Afro-American agricultural worker was one of the world's first proletarians in the construction of their culture, social structures, labor, and world view.

From the first generation of this new national minority group in America, there was a clear division in that world view. Before going on, one must remember that the only period when Black employment approached one hundred percent was during slavery, and since the end of World War II the number of Black unemployment soared. Poor Black people are the most brutally victimized and exploited sector; Black women were not considered a class, but their history cannot be explored properly in the same context with that of Black men. Reason being, capitalist patriarchy combined with racism shackled most Black women more firmly to the process of exploitation than any group of Black men. The highest stage of underdevelopment comes from the economically and social poor; and when everything is against them from the start, then what is expected of people to get out of poverty when they were driven into it. Poverty must be understood properly as a comparative relationship between the segment of classes; one deprived of basic human needs (e.g., food, shelter, clothing, and medical care) versus the most secure and affluent classes within a social and economic order. For many working-class whites, the Afro-American is less than a person and a more symbolic index between themselves and the abyss of absolute poverty. All Whites at every job level are the relative beneficiaries of racism in the labor force: the minorities of America's supply the basic draftees in the permanent and semi permanent reserve army of labor.

The demand for Black education has been the most enthusiastically supported political reform among Afro-American people from slavery till this present time. Unlike Black Capitalism, which appealed only to the Black entrepreneur and segments of the Black nationalist faction; the call for increase state support for Black educational institutions has been a universal concern among all classes. Less than ten percent of all former slaves in 1865 were literate. White racists from 1850s to 1960s saw the Blacks' demand for access to schools as a threat to the preservation of White supremacy. Free Blacks in the antebellum south who learned to read usually hid this explosive secret from their masters for obvious reasons. After the Civil War, Black women, men and children recognized the lack of education permanently restricted them to a life of an agricultural penury, and economic exploitation. Blacks knew that if they had the same education as Whites then they could get ahead in life, and that education at all levels was viewed as a decisive means to end the vicious of racial underdevelopment. Historically, the Black colleges is largely the direct product of racial segregation.

Ninety-one of the one hundred seven Black colleges were established before 1910. They were highly under financed and inadequately staffed; Black higher education was permitted to exist only as skeletal systems during the long fight of White supremacy. As late as 1946, only four Black colleges: Howard University, Fisk University, Talladega College and North Carolina State were accredited by the Association of American Universities. Although education was available to Blacks' after expanded educational legislation; it still was unequal to that of Whites', plus most Blacks could not afford it. The functions of Black college from the view of White society was to train the Blacks' to accept a separate and unequal position within American life. Despite these institutional barriers in quality education, the Black schools did a remarkable job in preparing their youth for productive careers in the natural sciences, social sciences, trades, and humanities. A major number of Black intellectuals during that era of segregation were: W.E.B. DuBois (sociologist), John Hope Franklin (historian), E. Franklin Frazier (sociologist), James Weldon Johnson (artists-novelists), Arna Bontemps (poet), Nikki Giovanni (poet, activist and educator), John Oliver Killens (taught creative-writing programs), and Frank Yerby (writer) all graduated from Fisk University along with many others in the twentieth century as decisive leaders in public policy.

One must remember that in a capitalist system such as America is the only thing that really counts is a how much wealth a person has, and within that wealth class racism still exist among those group of people. Oh yea, racism is still a big issue, but if you ask White people does it still exist; more than likely they will say it isn't a big problem while at the same time you got to watch out for the ones who speak first about the issue. There is a study that said at least a third of White people still raise their children to hate and or dislike Blacks and other minorities; because they do not want to let go of their traditions and still wants to have Black's genocide.

See, for me to mention genocide is to put everything into a reality of the thinking of the minority of Whites who and how they developed this system called capitalism for themselves and no one else. The most powerful thesis on the inevitability of Whites' genocide of Blacks was Sidney M. Willhem's "*Who Needs The Negro?*"

"The life situation of Black Americans deteriorates with the passing of each year ... technological efficiency makes possible the full realization of the nation's anti-Negro beliefs. The arrival of automation eliminates the need for Black labor, and racist values call for the Negro's removal from the American scene ... As the races pull apart into life styles with greater polarity, the Black ghetto evolves into the equivalent of the Indian reservation. What is the point, demands white America, in tolerating an unwanted racial minority when there is no economic necessity for acceptance, with machines now replacing human labor, who need the Blacks?"

This kind of thinking still exist today, but the problem is that the Whites' thought it was full proof. In recent years extreme racial polarization within the United States civil society accompanied by a pervading climate of fear and terrorism has reached into virtually every Black neighborhood. Many black institutions which were either developed in the brutal crucible of antebellum slavery or in the period of Jim Crow segregation are rapidly being destroyed. Two of these are the Black education systems, especially the traditional Black private and public colleges, and black-owned and operated businesses. A growing number of black workers become irrelevant to the U.S. economy and the level of unemployment for blacks under age 25 had reached staggering levels and continue to climb.

The Black race was and still is a victim of the greediness of the Elite Whites who are in control of this country, while keeping the majority of White Americans believing in the old traditions in a camouflaged way. The major under development tools used in Black communities has been and still is high unemployment, drugs, and alcohol-all in the control of Elite Whites. This is also true for some Whites who thought they were beyond losing the American dream have been bamboozled by the same Elite Whites. The sad irony is that certain sectors of White working class are also targeted for elimination and radical transformation. The identical process which threaten the Blacks' proletariat are confronting White autoworkers, steelworkers, rubber workers, textile workers, laborers, and many millions more. Whether White workers as a self-conscious mass will perceive that their own "benefits" from racism are only relative to the oppressed conditions of Black labor, and that the social and psychological image of the Blacks-as-inferior beings actually promotes their own exploitation as well as that of Blacks, cannot be predetermined. A majoritatian bloc against the New Right and the interest in capitalism at some first point call for the protracted culture and ideological transformation of the White working class. At least that is what most White working class is hoping for, but not realizing that it is all about money and not as much about the color of one's skin as it used to be. If the Elite Whites can get away with it, they are more willing to take care of their own for the survival of the White race.

Bibliography

"How Europe Underdeveloped Africa" by Walter Rodney with a postscript by A. M. Babu. Howard University Press, Washington, D. C. 1982.

"How Capitalism Underdeveloped Black America" by Manning Marable, South End Press, Boston, MA 1983 First edition sixth printing.

"Yurugu An African-centered Critique of European Cultural, Thought and Behavior" by Marimba Ani (Donna Richards).

Abstracts from the Sociology 102 Summer Course manual written and taught by Rev. Dr. Nikitah Okembe-RA Imani class 1996.

(2) "Whose Culture Do You Identify with Today?"

(Sociology 379 "African Intellectual Heritage" Part 3 "Culture and Identity" Author Ali A. Mazrui - Essay by Timothy L. Walker)

As the world turns on its axis, people are fighting to their death to keep their culture and identity because that's all they have that they can lay claim to. It's always someone who thinks they have the correct answer or method of doing things that messes up what the Creator has already put in place. In part three of the book African Intellectual Heritage: Towards Cultural Synthesis, Ali A. Mazrui writes about cultures and civilizations and how they are turned about to be as they are today. I agree with how Ali A. Mazrui defines culture and civilization, so I'll use his definitions and the stages of culture that he used as a working reference for my synthesis of part three with the focus of "Whose Culture Do You Identify with Today!"

Ali A. Mazrui defined culture "as a system of inter-related values, active enough to influence and condition perception, judgment, communication and behavior in a given society; and civilization as a culture which has endured, expanded, innovated and been elevated to new moral sensibilities." This definition is the essence of why humans were created, but something went wrong, and I will explain by using the stages of culture that Ali A. Mazrui wrote about.

The world that we live in puts people into color groups/boxes, with the main attraction being Black and White. This is the trick of the Enemy who has beguiled the White Elites into believing that whatever they say or do, others should govern themselves accordingly. This first took place when the Enemy/ Satan wanted to sit on the Mercy Seat and conned a third of God's children to follow him. God had and does have a perfect culture and civilization for His Children (Mankind), but when some were beguiled and disobeyed what the Creator had for them; He therefore took their original culture and civilization away from them.

Since the Katabole because of what happened in the para- graph above, the Enemy's next first contact to cause conflict and confusion was in the Garden of Eden with Adam and Eve. Note: Satan (The Enemy) knew that God's plan to restore Mankind (His Children) back to their perfect culture and civilization was to come through His Savior by way of Adam and Eve to set forth the inheritance for all mankind. When a person or people has a conflict, they become confused and start to ask irrational questions, so I have to think that Adam and Eve asked themselves after they knew they were naked (physically and spiritually), Whose culture are we to identify with now and what will our civilization be like? That is a dangerous question for anyone to ask themselves, but it's reality, because it's been happening ever since then. It's a divine law that positive and negative do not go together, so eventually one will conquer the other, and that's where we are today, especially pertaining to the Black and White issues concerning culture (s), civilization (s), and who's right or wrong.

Ideally it really would be nice if Black and White people could live side by side in harmony and peace, but time and history have proven that their diverse natures are not compatible, mostly because Whites lack respect for Black people. Whenever the chemistry of the two are forced into proximity, the results are volatile. For example, the African and European diametrical approach to life, death, and sexuality are very different, just as the cross was originally a symbol of life to Black people but became a symbol of death to White people and is now a graveyard ornament in western society.

The White Elites have changed the cultures of most people they have encountered. This has been done by any means necessary, but most of all they have erased and rewritten and are still writing history as though they are the chosen one of the Creator and without them there would be nothing. Since they control the media in all aspects, it is easy for people who have nothing or little to ask, who am I really and where did I come from? Those who don't know the answer to that question need to do some serious research, because the true history is beneath all the lies that have been told. Once you find the truth, you must be willing to do something with it; if not, what's the use of finding the truth in the first place? The truth will set your Soul free and allow the Spirit of the Creator to rise up in you, and then you can live Life as it was intended from the beginning.

Jesus Christ said in John 10:10 (KJV), "the thief cometh not, but to steal, and to kill, and to destroy I come that they might have life, and that they might have it more abundantly." The Elites are the thieves of the world, who have done all these things, especially to Black people, but will be last and that which is last will be first. an order, and now things are out of order. So, until all cultures and civilizations are reunited and returned to their original people, it is a man's responsibility to make the journey through research to get back what has been taken from them. I think this is the only way we can identify with our Creator.

Within part three of "African Intellectual Heritage," I read how some great African and African-American thinkers thought Black people were to overcome diversity of cultures and get back their true identity. After reading their thoughts, I had come to some conclusions that if Black people in earlier years had gotten together as a whole, then we would not be in the situation we're in today (and still believe it true today). I know that the Creator created every human being with their own personality that identifies, but within that, we are to identify with the culture which we were made for, not forced into.

I think if Black people would take the advice and ideals of W.E.B. DuBois and Booker T. Washington, and the mentality of Marcus M. Garvey and put them all together rationally, and then Black people can be economically and politically sound within this nation. These three amongst others were before their time, but they left something for those who have the heart to stand for what's rightfully theirs, and that's their true cultural heritage that has been set before them by their original ancestors.

My ancestors were of high cultural civilizations before contact with other cultures and then conflicts that led to conquest. This conquest has kept Black people confused, and it beguiled their soul, spirit, and body. Since the destruction of Black people, especially in the United States, we tend to go through culture revivals, but it does not last, because the elites have figured out a way to keep us off the trail toward the true meaning of being Black. W.E.B. DuBois said that "if Black people were to get the best education possible, learn how the elites live and think, then the Blacks who accomplish that could pass it on to their fellow Blacks, and use what they learn about the elites, against the elites." Booker T. Washington said, "Blacks have to learn and prefect what they have already working for them in order to survive, for example farming and building things.

We know that doesn't work, because just the other day in the newspaper the Black farmers are complaining to the government about unequal lending practices towards Black people. This has been going on since share cropping, which is another form of slavery?"

The reason W.E.B. DuBois thought the way he did was because he was raised in New England and educated in an Ivy League school, while Booker T. Washington came from the South, born of slaves, therefore, they had different backgrounds and cultures. I think it could have worked then and even more so now because there is more opportunity for Black people to achieve what they have always wanted to do as a people. Also if those who do get or have gotten the high level of education do not forget that they are Black, and coincide with those who have perfected the necessary skills to build and farm, then Blacks will have started an economic base that's needed for survival. While doing this both groups mentioned above have to pass on what they have learned to those who are lacking, and when this happens with the mentality of a Marcus Garvey, then Blacks will be on their way as being one people who shall not fall. As long as there is a division, then half the battle plan of the Elites has been accomplished.

In order for Blacks to fight effectively against their enemy in the flesh, who happens to be those who practice White Supremacy, we have to learn our true history about ourselves. For example: Black African culture set for the whole world an example of extraordinary vitality and vigor. All vitalized conceptions, religious as well as philosophies, came from that source. The average Black person cannot grasp that, because they have been taught that everything that came into existence was because of the White man. That is a lie straight from the pits of hell, and our thinking has to be at a higher level than reversing what the White man has used against us, and be as our ancestors were. Once Black people have the truth about themselves, the next step is to make some good of it; they too are to keep asking themselves the question, Whose culture are they today and then move forward with the truth? I quote Marcus Garvey in saying, "except the individual, the nation or the race has the power that is exclusive, it means that individual, race or nation will be bound by the will of another ... man is not satisfied or moved by prayers or petitions, but every man is moved by the power of authority which forces him to do even against his will."

I think that's a true statement, but for it to work we as Black people have to have that Spirit Creator working on the inside of us, because everything that happens first happens in the spirit realm. In the Bible Jesus said in Matthew 18:18 (KJV), "Verily I say unto you, Whatsoever ye shall bind on earth shall be bound in heaven: and whatsoever ye shall loose on earth shall be loosed in heaven," meaning we have the power and authority to control what happens to us while we are in our flesh bodies. The Apostle Paul wrote, "For we wrestle not against flesh and blood, but against principalities, against powers, against the rulers of the darkness of this world, against spiritual wickedness in high places" Ephesians 6:12 (KJV). If Black people as a whole can grasp the revelation behind what Jesus Christ said and what the Apostle Paul wrote, then we won't have to ask that question about our culture, because it will come alive. We have to have FAITH in what has been said and put it into action, because "Faith without Works is Dead," We as black people have been dead spiritually for a long time, and this has affected our walk in the flesh; so what Marcus Garvey said could become a reality, but we as Black people have to make it happen. It can happen. Remember Black Wall Street in Tulsa, Oklahoma? It was no joke, but in order to reach that platform again black people must support one another in all their ventures, and be courageous regardless of the situation. As the saying goes, history will repeat itself, but the reality and irony of history is that it doesn't have to have the same script.

Don't surrender your Culture, Civilization or Identity for anyone!

(3) "How Was Your Sleep Last Night?" by Timothy L. Walker

I believe that time spent sleeping and being at rest is our most important part of our daily life cycle. I heard and read somewhere that "humans on the average spend most of their time sleeping, and at a minimum, we should get at least eight hours of continuous sleep in a twenty-four-hour period in order for us to function properly for that next day." We as humans have abused that so call thought, because we don't know who's in control and what's involved in our sleep, most people just sleep because they are tired and have a total blackout of their dreams because of that. I divide the twenty-four-hour daily life cycle into three eight-hour increments; eight hours of sleep, eight hours of employment to survive in this world system, and eight hours for our families and church.

I also believe that sleep is the most important, because when we sleep our most inner thought-s are manifested within our hearts and minds, and if we are not sleeping with Jesus; then the time we spend sleeping is lost forever. If we let the Word of God minister and work on, in and through our hearts and minds while we are asleep as well as awoke, then think how much better our lives will be and how much better we will feel towards everybody we come in contact within our everyday walk. Have you had your daily Breath of Life from God today other than by His Grace that you are Alive? {Genesis 2:7 (KJV)} Paul writes in I Thessalonians 4: 13-15 (KJV) says "But I would not have you to be ignorant, brethren, concerning them which are asleep, that ye sorrow not, even as others which have no hope. For if we believe that Jesus died and rose again, even so them also which sleep in Jesus, will God bring with him." For this we say unto you by the Word of the Lord, that we which are alive and remain unto the coming of the Lord shall not prevent them which are asleep." Paul is referring to "them which are asleep and sleep in Jesus" as the physically dead in Christ and for everyone who is a Believer and Christian has this Inheritance of Eternal Life, for You Giving their Life back to Jesus. {John 5: 24 (KJV), Romans 5: 20-21 (KJV), and Romans 8: 2 (KJV)} I'm going to refer to asleep as those who are not saved (not born again) are of the world, because they are asleep - asleep concerning the things of God and of The Kingdom of God.{Romans 10:3 (KJV)}

There are Christians walking around spiritually dead in Christ; not aware that the Kingdom of God in Eternity will be on earth. Why? Because they don't have enough Faith to believe that such a thing will be and maybe because what's being taught is the hinder of the Kingdom/Church that could be "right now!" Genesis 2:17 (KJV). They too are asleep, remain in darkness, but saved by His Grace; "if they endure until the end" because they had confessed with their mouth that Jesus Christ is their Lord and Savior and died for their sins Matthew 10: 32 (KJV), and Romans 10: 9-14 (KJV)

Notes

Replacing "Believe" with "Faith" and it still means the same thing. Don't let us forget that at that moment when we made that confession with our mouth, we are called to the ministry to minister (work) as Jesus did in Mark 10:45 (KJV).

This is not to say everyone is called or going to be a Minister/Pastor. Paul reminds us, that we as Christians need to learn how to "pray without ceasing" I Thessalonians 5: 17 (KJV). Pray without ceasing in a manner that it does not hinder your functions to sleep, work and perform your daily commitments unto your family and church and everything that comes to mind in accordance with the Word of God.

When we come together on Sundays and have Church, meaning come to Praise and Worship the Lord Jesus Christ for what He has done and what He has promised He would do for You, Your family and Us as the Church In His Image. (If you didn't know it, that's part of "Kingdom Business," and that is when you should let it all hang out. Be "Decent and In Order," the world does it just the opposite way on Friday nights after getting paid, we already got paid because Jesus Gave His Life a Ransom for Many. {Mark 10: 45 (KJV), Matthew 20:28 (KJV), and *Philippians 2:4-16 (KJV)}

Note

Notice it did not say Ransom for All, Ransom for Many.

If you've been there, then you know what I'm talking about, or you have heard or seen it for yourself, you be some kind of tired the next day without that sleep, that time you missed sleeping was God's time and if we didn't realize it, it's the best time for Jesus to minister to You. {Leviticus 26:6 (KJV)} I believe sleep and being at rest is the most enjoyable and part of our daily life cycle, and with continuous praying in some form of fashion during the twenty-four-hour cycle of life will give us our rest while we sleep, don't forget that when we sleep or rest as others do, it's the best time for the Thief (Devil/Satan) to come. {Genesis 41: 8 &16 (KJV)} The best time for a thief to steal you of something is in the dark, it's in their best interest because it's hard for a person to identified them, so Satan's best offense is at night and for us to see, we need some sort of Light, and when we sleep as Christians, sleep with Jesus, for He is our Light in that time of darkness to prepare our steps for the next day, so we can shine before the world. Matthew 5: 14 &16 (KJV), John 8: 12 (KJV), John 12: 35-36, 50 (KJV), and II Corinthians 6:14 (KJV)

I Thessalonians 5: 2-6 (KJV) says "For yourselves know perfectly that the day of the Lord so cometh as a thief in the night. For when they shall say, Peace and safety; then sudden destruction cometh upon them, as travail upon a woman with child; and they shall not escape. But ye, brethren!, are not in darkness, that, that day should overtake you as a thief Ye are all the children of light, and the children of the day: we are not of the night, nor of darkness. Therefore let us not sleep, as do others; but let us watch and be sober." The word sober here is not only referring to be sober from alcohol and drugs and anything that fix into that category or do harm to the Body of Christ physically and mentally, but also as Christians be not angry, bitter or have hatred in our hearts and minds when we sleep, because if we do these things, we're not sleeping with Jesus, and without the proper sleep, how can we function properly for the next 16 hours that are before us to have a complete meaningful day." I Peter 5: 8 (KJV), Psalm 3:5 (KJV), and Proverbs 3: 24-26 (KJV)

Okay here's something else to think about, I Thessalonians 5: 7-10 (KJV) says "For they that sleep, sleep in the night; and they that be drunken (of the world) are drunken in the night. But let us, who are of the day, be sober, putting on the breastplate of faith and love; and the helmet, the hope of salvation. For God hath not appointed us to wrath, but to obtain salvation by our Lord Jesus Christ, who died for us, that, whether we wake or sleep, we should live together with him." I have not found in the Bible where it says take off any part of the Whole Armor of God, so don't take it off while sleeping, it protects you and I spiritually for the Warfare. We prepare ourselves to fight the Good fight of Faith and taking back dominion, and when we start Taking Dominion that's rightfully ours as Christians and Believers of Jesus Christ being our Lord and Savior, then be ready for a fight. Revelation 1: 5-6 (KJV)

When we walk in this world among the unsaved and after a good night's sleep with Jesus, we should able to do the things that Paul wrote about in II Corinthians 6: 14 (KJV), and I Thessalonians 5: 14 -22 (KJV) on a daily basis, practice makes perfect and the more we do these things on a daily basis, the more we'll be able to walk within the anointing God has for us. The more we perfect our Faith, Walk & Work too perfection concerning God's Kingdom Business, likewise, the more power Jesus will release to us through His Holy Spirit, it's all according to our Faith which guides our walk and work in Life; so as time passes us by before we sleep again, let's ask ourselves this question; Did I greet everyone with a holy kiss from God today? I Thessalonians 5: 26 (KJV) and Romans 16: 16 (KJV)

Paul writes "I charge you by the Lord that this epistle be read unto all the holy brethren" I Thessalonians 5:27 (KJV), so to understand more of what I'm saying, read the First Epistle of Thessalonians and the other Books I have used. Now, I have done my part and I hope that you read the Word of God with a better understanding and outlook in what I have written; it could be a blessing to You and for those who you share with, so take it as Grace from our Lord Jesus Christ and let Him be with You at all times.

Now I can propose this question: If we are not sleeping with and in Jesus, then who are we sleeping with?

The next four Subtitles {**Reconstruction Era, Jim Crow, Black Wall Street, and Christianity and the Negro Race**} will show how the White Elites and Satan (who has to work through the Powerful of the Majority) has worked the **Four Horns** against the Black race and People of Color.

The majority of white people then and now and just because of the color of their skin, but the Truth of the matter is that the elites and Satan don't give a damn about them either, but needed a Pawn to help them succeed.

(a.) "Reconstruction Era"

Reconstruction addressed how the eleven seceding states would regain what the Constitution calls a "republican form of government" and be reseated in Congress, the civil status of the former leaders of the Confederacy, and the Constitutional and legal status of freedmen, especially their civil rights and whether they should be given the right to vote. Intense controversy erupted throughout the South over these issues. The laws and constitutional amendments that laid the foundation for the most radical phase of Reconstruction were adapted from 1866 to 1871. By the 1870s, Reconstruction had officially provided freedmen with equal rights under the constitution, and blacks were voting and taking political office. Republican legislatures, coalitions of whites and blacks, established the first public school systems and numerous charitable institutions in the South.

Freedmen and the Enactment of the Black Codes

Southern state governments quickly enacted the restrictive "Black Codes." However, they were abolished in 1866 and seldom had an effect, because the Freedmen's Bureau (not the local courts) handled the legal affairs of freedmen. The Black Codes indicated the plans of the southern whites for the former slaves. [1] The freedmen would have more rights than did free blacks before the war, but they still had only a limited set of second-class civil rights, no voting rights, and no citizenship. They could not own firearms, serve on a jury in a lawsuit involving whites, or move about without employment. [2] The Black Codes outraged northern opinion. They were overthrown by the Civil Rights Act of 1866 that gave the freedmen full legal equality (except for the right to vote). [3] The freedmen, with the strong backing of the Freedmen's Bureau, rejected gang-labor work patterns that had been used in slavery. Instead of gang labor, freed people preferred family-based labor groups. [4] They forced planters to bargain for their labor. Such bargaining soon led to the establishment of the system of sharecropping, which gave the freedmen greater economic independence and social autonomy than gang labor. However, because they lacked capital, and the planters continued to own the means of production (tools, draft animals, and land), the freedmen were forced into producing cash crops (mainly cot- ton) for the land-owners and merchants, and they entered into a crop-lien system. Widespread poverty, disruption to an agricultural economy too dependent on cotton, and the falling price of cotton led within decades to the routine indebtedness of the majority of the freedmen, and poverty by many planners. [5] Northern officials gave varying reports on conditions for the freedmen in the South. One harsh assessment came from Carl Schurz, who reported on the situation in the states along the Gulf Coast. His report documented dozens of extra-judicial killings and claimed that hundreds or thousands more African-Americans were killed. [6]

References: [1] Donald, Civil War and Reconstruction (2001), Ch. 31. [2] Oberholtzer 1:128–9. [3] Jump up Donald (2001), p. 527. [4] Hunter, p. 67. [5] Barney, The Passage of the Republic, p. 251, pp. 284–286. [6] Report on the Condition of the South / Schurz, Carl, 1829–1906.

African-American Officeholders

Republicans took control of all southern state governorships and state legislatures, except for Virginia. [1] The Republican coalition elected numerous African-Americans to local, state, and national offices; though they did not dominate any electoral offices, black men as representatives voting in state and federal legislatures marked a drastic social change. At the beginning of 1867, no African-American in the South held political office, but within three or four years about 15 percent of the officeholders in the South were black—a larger proportion than in 1990. [2] In **1860** blacks were the majority of the population in Mississippi and South Carolina, 47 percent in Louisiana, 45 percent in Alabama, and 44 percent in Georgia and Florida, [3] so their political influence was still far less than their percentage of the population. About 137 black officeholders had lived outside the South before the Civil War. Some who had escaped from slavery to the North and had become educated returned to help the South advance in the postwar era. Others were free blacks before the war, who had achieved education and positions of leadership elsewhere. Other African-American men who served were already leaders in their communities, including a number of preachers. As happened in white communities, not all leadership depended upon wealth and literacy. [4]

References: [1] Georgia had a Republican governor and legislature, but the Republican hegemony was tenuous at best, and Democrats continued to win presidential elections there. See 1834 March 28 article in "This Day in Georgia History" compiled by Ed Jackson and Charles Pou; cf. Rufus Bullock. [2] McPherson, James M. (1992). Abraham Lincoln and the "Second American Revolution." Oxford University Press. p.19. ISBN 978-0-19-507606-6. [3] "Date of Secession Compared to 1860 Black Population," America's Civil War website, accessed 9 April 2014. [4] Foner 1988, Ch. 7; Foner, "Freedom's Lawmakers," introduction. and Steven Hahn, "A Nation Under Our Feet."

White paramilitary organizations, especially the "Ku Klux Klan" and the "White League and Red Shirts" formed with the political aim of driving out the Republicans. They also disrupted political organizing and terrorized blacks to bar them from the polls. Passage of the 13th, 14th, and 15th Amendments is the constitutional legacy of Reconstruction. These Reconstruction Amendments established the rights that led to Supreme Court rulings in the mid-20th century that struck down school segregation. A Second Reconstruction, sparked by the Civil Rights Movement, led to civil rights laws in 1964 and 1965 that ended segregation and opened the polls to blacks. **Hum—on paper only (Poll Taxes and other distractions); just as bad as it is now!**

There were few African-Americans elected or appointed to national office, and African-Americans voted for both white and black candidates. The Fifteenth Amendment to the United States Constitution guaranteed only that voting could not be restricted on the basis of race, color, or previous condition of servitude. From 1868 on, campaigns and elections were surrounded by violence as white insurgents and paramilitary tried to suppress the black vote, and fraud was rampant. Many Congressional elections in the South were contested. Even states with majority African-American population often elected only one or two African-American representatives to Congress. Exceptions included South Carolina; at the end of Reconstruction, four of its five Congressmen were African American.

Example of the Religion and Economic Horns

Under organized religion freedmen were very active in forming their own churches, mostly Baptist or Methodist, and giving their ministers both moral and political leadership roles. In a process of self-segregation, practically all blacks left white churches so that few racially integrated congregations remained (apart from some Catholic churches in Louisiana).

Four main groups competed with each other across the South to form new Methodist churches composed of freedmen. They were the African Methodist Episcopal Church; the African Methodist Episcopal Zion Church; the Colored Methodist Episcopal Church (which was sponsored by the white Methodist Episcopal Church, South) and the well-funded Methodist Episcopal Church (Northern white Methodists). [1] By 1871 the Northern Methodists had 88,000 black members in the South, and had opened numerous schools for them. [2] Blacks in the South were a core element of the Republican Party, and their ministers had powerful political roles that were distinctive since they did not depend on white support, in contrast to teachers, politicians, businessmen, and tenant farmers. [3] Acting on the principle as stated by Charles H. Pearce, an AME minister in Florida: A man in this State cannot do his whole duty as a minister except he looks out for the political interests of his people, over 100 black ministers were elected to state legislatures during Reconstruction, as well as several to Congress and one, Hiram Revels, to the U.S. Senate. [4] In a highly controversial move, the Northern Methodists used the Army to seize control of Methodist churches in large cities, over the vehement protests of the Southern Methodists. Historian Ralph Morrow reports: "A War Department order of November 1863, applicable to the Southwestern states of the Confederacy, authorized the Northern Methodists to occupy all houses of worship belonging to the Methodist Episcopal Church South in which a loyal minister, appointed by a loyal bishop of said church, does not officiate." [5] Across the North most evangelical denominations, especially the Methodists, Congregationalists, and Presbyterians, as well as the Quakers, were strong supporters of radical policies. The focus on social problems paved the way for the Social Gospel movement. Matthew Simpson, a Methodist Bishop, played a leading role in mobilizing the Northern Methodists for the cause. His biographer calls him the "High Priest of the Radical Republicans." [6] The Methodist Ministers Association of Boston, meeting two weeks after Lincoln's assassination, called for a hard line against the Confederate leadership: Resolved, that no terms should be made with traitors, no compromise with rebels... That we hold the National authority bound by the most solemn obligation to God and man to bring all the civil and military leaders of the rebellion to trial by due course of law, and when they are clearly convicted, to execute them. [7] The denominations all sent missionaries, teachers, and activists to the South to help the Freedmen. Only the Methodists made many converts, however. [8] Activists sponsored by the Northern Methodist Church played a major role in the Freedmen's Bureau, notably in such key educational roles as the Bureau's state superintendent or assistant superintendent of education for Virginia, Florida, Alabama, and South Carolina. [9] Many Americans interpreted great events in religious terms. Historian Wilson Fallin contrasts the interpretation of Civil War and Reconstruction in white versus black Baptist sermons in Alabama. White Baptists expressed the view that: "God had chastised them and given them a special mission—to maintain orthodoxy, strict Biblicism, personal piety, and traditional race relations. Slavery, they insisted, had not been sinful. Rather, emancipation was a historical tragedy and the end of Reconstruction was a clear sign of God's favor. In sharp contrast, Black Baptists interpreted the Civil War, emancipation and Reconstruction as: God's gift of freedom. They appreciated opportunities to exercise their independence, to worship in their own way, to affirm their worth and dignity, and to proclaim the fatherhood of God and the brotherhood of man. Most of all, they could form their own churches, associations, and conventions. These institutions offered self-help and racial uplift and provided places where the gospel of liberation could be proclaimed. As a result, black preachers continued to insist that God would protect and help them; God would be their rock in a stormy land." **[10]**

References: [1] Daniel W. Stowell (1998). Rebuilding Zion: The Religious Reconstruction of the South, 1863–1877. Oxford UP. pp. 83–84; and Clarence Earl Walker, A Rock in a Weary Land: The African Methodist Episcopal Church During the Civil War and Reconstruction (1982). [2] William W. Sweet, "The Methodist Episcopal Church and Reconstruction," Journal of the Illinois State Historical Society (1914) 7#3 pp. 147–165 JSTOR 40194198 at p.157. [3] Donald Lee Grant (1993). The Way It Was in the South: The Black Experience in Georgia. U. of Georgia Press. p. 264. [4] Foner, Reconstruction, (1988) p. 93 [5] Ralph E. Morrow, "Northern Methodism in the South during Reconstruction," Mississippi Valley Historical Review (1954) 41#2 pp. 197–218, quote on p. 202 JSTOR 1895802; Ralph E. Morrow, Northern Methodism and Reconstruction (1956), and Stowell, Rebuilding Zion: The Religious Reconstruction of the South, 1863–1877, pp. 30–31. [6] Robert D. Clark, The Life of Matthew Simpson (1956) pp. 245–67. [7] Fredrick A. Norwood, ed., Sourcebook of American Methodism (1982) p. 323; William W. Sweet, "The Methodist Episcopal Church and Reconstruction," Journal of the Illinois State Historical Society (1914) 7#3 pp. 147–165, quote on p. 161 JSTOR 40194198 [8] Victor B. Howard, Religion and the Radical Republicans Movement, 1860–1870 (1990) pp. 212–13. [9] Morrow (1954) p. 205. [10] Wilson Fallin Jr., Uplifting the People: Three Centuries of Black Baptists in Alabama (2007) pp. 52–53.

Example of the Education Horn

Education: Public schools according to historian James D. Anderson argued that the freed slaves were the first Southerners "to campaign for universal, state-supported public education." **[1]** Blacks in the Republican coalition played a critical role in establishing the principle in state constitutions for the first time during congressional Reconstruction. Some slaves had learned to read from white playmates or colleagues before formal education were allowed by law; African-Americans started "native schools" before the end of the war. Sabbath schools were another widespread means that freedmen developed to teach literacy. [2] When they gained suffrage, black politicians took this commitment to public education to state constitutional conventions. The Republicans created a system of public schools, which were segregated by race everywhere except New Orleans. Generally, elementary and a few secondary schools were built in most cities, and occasionally in the countryside, but the South had few cities. [3] The rural areas faced many difficulties opening and maintaining public schools. In the country, the public school was often a one-room affair that attracted about half the younger children. The teachers were poorly paid, and their pay was often in arrears. Conservatives contended the rural schools were too expensive and unnecessary for a region where the vast majority of people were cotton or tobacco farmers. They had no vision of a better future for their residents. One historian found that the schools were less effective than they might have been because "poverty, the inability of the states to collect taxes, and inefficiency and corruption in many places prevented successful operation of the schools."

After Reconstruction ended, and the Whites disfranchised the Blacks and imposed Jim Crow, they consistently under funded Black Institutions, including the schools. After the war, northern missionaries founded numerous private academies and colleges across the South for freedmen. In addition, every state founded state colleges for freedmen, such as Alcorn State University in Mississippi. The normal schools and state colleges produced generations of teachers who were integral to the education of African-American children under the segregated system. By the end of the century, the majority of African-Americans were literate.

In the late 19th century, the federal government established land grant legislation to provide funding for higher education across the United States. Learning that blacks were excluded from land-grant colleges in the South, in 1890, the federal government insisted that southern states establish black state institutions as land-grant colleges to provide for black higher education, in order to continue to receive funds for their already established white schools. Some states classified their black state colleges as land-grant institutions. Former Congressman John Roy Lynch wrote, "There are very many liberals, fair-minded and influential Democrats in the State [Mississippi] who are strongly in favor of having the State provide for the liberal education of both races." [4]

References: [1] James D. Anderson (1988). The Education of Blacks in the South, 1860–1935. U of North Carolina Press. p. 4. **[2]** Anderson, The Education of Blacks in the South, 1860–1935 (1988), pp. 6–15. **[3]** Tyack and Lowe. **"The Constitutional Moment: Reconstruction and Black Education in the South."** (1986): and William Preston Vaughn, Schools for All: The Blacks and Public Education in the South, 1865–1877 (University Press of Kentucky, 2015). **[4]** B. D. Mayberry, A Century of Agriculture in the 1890 Land-Grant Institutions and Tuskegee University, 1890–1990 (1992).

(b.) "Jim Crow"

The term came to be a derogatory epithet for African-Americans and a designation for their segregated life. From the late 1870s, southern state legislatures, no longer controlled by carpetbaggers and freedmen, passed laws requiring the separation of whites from *persons-of-color* in public transportation and schools. Generally, anyone of ascertainable or strongly suspected black ancestry in any degree was for that purpose a *person- of-color*; the pre-Civil War distinction favoring those whose ancestry was known to be mixed particularly the half-French *free-persons-of-color* in Louisiana was abandoned. The segregation principle was extended to parks, cemeteries, theaters, and restaurants in an effort to prevent any contact between *Blacks* and *Whites* as equals. It was codified on local and state levels and most famously with the "separate but equal" decision of the U.S. Supreme Court in Plessy v. Ferguson (1896).

In 1954 the Supreme Court reversed Plessy in Brown v. Board of Education of Topeka. It declared segregation in public schools unconstitutional, and, by extension, that ruling was applied to other public facilities. In the years following, subsequent decisions struck down similar kinds of Jim Crow legislation. These Jim Crow laws followed the 1800–1866 Black Codes, which had previously restricted the civil rights and civil liberties of African-Americans. Segregation of public (state-sponsored) schools was declared unconstitutional by the Supreme Court of the United States in 1954 in Brown v. Board of Education; although in some cases it took years for this decision to be acted on. Generally, the remaining Jim Crow laws were overruled by the Civil Rights Act of 1964 and the Voting Rights Act of 1965, but years of action and court challenges were needed to unravel numerous means of institutional discrimination.

As described in section "A" of the Reconstruction Era in the 1870s, Democrats gradually regained power in the southern legislatures by using paramilitary groups (White League and Red Shirts) to disrupt Republican organizing and run Republican officeholders out of town, and intimidate blacks to suppress their voting. Extensive voter fraud and increasing violence against blacks during campaigns from 1868 and onward helped the national Democratic Party compromise to gain southern support in the presidential election resulted in the government's withdrawing the last of the federal troops from the South. White Democrats had regained political power in every southern state, and these southern White Democratic Redeemer governments legislated Jim Crow laws, officially segregating Black people from the white population.

Blacks were still elected to local offices through the 1880s, but the establishment Democrats were passing laws to make voter registration and electoral rules more restrictive, with the result that political participation by most Blacks and many poor Whites began to decrease. Between 1890 and 1910, ten of the eleven former Confederate states, starting with Mississippi, passed new constitutions or amendments that effectively disenfranchised most Blacks and tens of thousands of poor Whites through a combination of poll taxes, literacy and comprehension tests, and residency and record-keeping requirements.

Grandfather clauses temporarily permitted some illiterate Whites to vote but gave no relief to most Blacks. Those who could not vote were not eligible to serve on juries and could not run for local offices. They effectively disappeared from political life, as they could not influence the state legislatures, and their interests were overlooked. While public schools had been established by Reconstruction legislatures for the first time in most southern states, those four Black children were consistently under-funded compared to schools for White children, even when considered within the strained finances of the postwar South, where the decreasing price of cotton kept the agricultural economy at a low. Like schools, Jim Crow public libraries were under-funded and often stocked with secondhand books and other resources. These facilities were not introduced for African-Americans in the South until the first decade of the 20th century.

Throughout Jim Crow, the libraries were only available sporadically. Prior to the twentieth century, most libraries established for African-Americans where school-library combi- nations. Many public libraries for both European and African- American patrons at this period were founded as the result of middle-class activism aided by matching grants from the Carnegie Foundation. In some cases, progressive measures intended to reduce election fraud, such as the Eight Box Law in South Carolina, acted against black and white voters who were illiterate, as they could not follow the directions. While the separation of African-Americans from the general population was becoming legalized and formalized during the Progressive Era (1890s -1920s), it was also becoming customary. For instance, even in cases in which Jim Crow laws did not expressly forbid Black people to participate in sports or recreation, a segregated culture had become common.

In the Jim Crow context, the presidential election of 1912 was steeply slanted against the interests of Black Americans. Most Blacks still lived in the South, where they had been effectively disfranchised, so they could not vote at all. While poll taxes and literacy requirements banned many poor or illiterate Americans from voting, these stipulations frequently had loopholes that exempted European-Americans from meeting the requirements. In Oklahoma, for instance, anyone qualified to vote before 1866, or related to someone qualified to vote before 1866 (a kind of "grandfather clause") was exempted from the literacy requirement; the only persons who could vote before that year were European male Americans. European-Americans were effectively exempted from the literacy testing, whereas Black Americans were effectively singled out by the law.

White southerners resented Black Americans, who rep- resented the Confederacy's Civil War defeat: With White Supremacy challenged throughout the South, many Whites sought to protect their former status by threatening African- Americans who exercised their new rights. White Democrats used their power to segregate public spaces and facilities in law and reestablish social dominance over blacks in the South. One rationale for the systematic exclusion of Black Americans from southern public society was that it was for their own protection. An early 20th-century scholar suggested that allowing blacks in white schools would mean constantly subjecting them to adverse feeling and opinion, which might lead to a morbid race consciousness. This perspective took anti- black sentiment for granted, because bigotry was widespread in the South after slavery became a racial caste.

After World War II, African-Americans increasingly challenged segregation, as they believed they had more than earned the right to be treated as full citizens because of their military service and sacrifices. The Civil Rights Movement was energized by a number of flashpoints, including the 1946 blinding of World War II veteran Isaac Woodard while he was in U.S. Army uniform (Isaac Woodard from Wikipedia, the free encyclopedia https://en.wikipedia.org/wiki/Isaac_Woodard), and in 1948 President Harry S. Truman issued Executive Order 9981, desegregating the armed services. As the Civil Rights Movement gained momentum and used federal courts to attack Jim Crow statutes, the European-dominated governments of many of the southern states countered by passing alternative forms of restrictions.

The NAACP Legal Defense Committee (a group that became independent of the NAACP) and its lawyer, Thurgood Marshall brought the landmark case Brown v. Board of Education of Topeka, 347 U.S. 483 (1954) before the Supreme Court. In its pivotal 1954 decision, the Court unanimously overturned the 1896 Plessy decision. The Supreme Court found that legally mandated (de jure) public school segregation was unconstitutional. The decision had far-reaching social ramifications. De jure segregation was not ended until the passage of the Civil Rights Act of 1964.

History has shown that problems of educating poor children are not confined to minority status, and states and cities have continued to grapple with approaches. court ruling did not stop De Facto or residentially based school segregation. Such segregation continues today in many regions. Some city school systems have also begun to focus on issues of economic and class segregation rather than racial segregation, as they have found that problems are more prevalent when the children of the poor of any ethnic group are concentrated.

In 2012, civil rights advocate Michelle Alexander argued in her book, The New Jim Crow, that America's war on drugs, which disproportionately affects African-Americans, has produced new discrimination comparable to that of the Jim Crow laws. She says that, by treating black criminals more harshly than white criminals, and decimating communities of color, the U.S. criminal justice system functions as a contemporary system of racial control relegating millions to a permanent second-class status even as it formally adheres to the principle of colorblindness. Fast-forward to 2016, and that same thinking is still strong, actions are sugarcoated, and there are some "People-of-Color" who play into the very hand that will smack them down? Now after the 2016 elections, the code words of "Let's Make America Great Again" will be in full force with a lot of "sugar" sprinkled on the actions that go forth. My suggestion to all who are not Elites, regardless of the color of your skin, is to be "Watchmen and Watchwomen" as God had commanded His people to do.

(c.) "Black Wall Street"

This is one that's not in most of White America's history books, nor in the current editions of the World of Encyclopedia under the heading of riots, Oklahoma, and "Tulsa race riot of 1921" because White America wants everyone to believe that Black people have always had and still have to depend on them to even sustain life or get ahead.

The story begins when many Black Americans moved to Oklahoma in the years before Oklahoma became a state and after it became a state in 1907. Oklahoma for many black people represented a change and provided them a chance to get away from slavery, Jim Crow, and the Black Code and whatever else the Whites/Elites had in store for them with their harsh racism of their previous homes. They traveled there by wagons, horses, trains, and even on foot because they were determined to better themselves; plus they had ancestors who could be traced back to Oklahoma when it was just a territory.

After the Emancipation Proclamation, Oklahoma was just a territory and many black people could live freely there; in addition, some had been adopted by the various Muskogee speaking peoples, such Creeks, Seminoles, and the Yuchi Indian tribes and it was mentioned that it would be a black and Indian state. When Tulsa, Oklahoma, became a booming, well-noted town in the United States, many people considered it to be two separate cities rather than one city of united communities. The White residents of Tulsa referred to the area north of the Frisco railroad tracks as Little Africa, and this community later acquired the name Greenwood and was home to about 10,000 Black residents in 1921. Greenwood was centered on a street known as Greenwood Avenue. This street was important because it ran north for over a mile from the Frisco Railroad yards, and it was one of the few streets that did not cross through both Black and White neighborhoods. The citizens of Greenwood took pride in this fact because it was something they had all to themselves and did not have to share with the white community of Tulsa. Greenwood Avenue was the home of the Black Americans Commercial District with many redbrick buildings. These buildings belonged to Black Americans, and they had thriving businesses, including grocery stores, banks, libraries, and much more. Greenwood was one of the most affluent communities and that's how it became known as "Black Wall Street."

The best description of "Black Wall Street" would be like a mini-Beverly Hills. It was the golden door of the Black community during the early 1900s, and it proved that African-Americans had a successful infrastructure. That's what Black Wall Street was all about. The dollar circulated 36 to 100 times, sometimes taking a year for currency to leave the community, but now a dollar leaves the Black community in fifteen minutes, if not faster. Whites/Elites hated the thought that Black people were doing so great, especially without their help, and they had to destroy Black Wall Street, one of the most affluent all-Black communities in America. When the lower economic Europeans looked over and saw what the Black community had created, many of them were jealous; so mobs of envious Whites (the impetus behind it all was the infamous Ku Klux Klan, working in concert with ranking city officials and many other sympathizers) bombed Greenwood from the air and burned it to the ground in less than twelve hours. A once thriving thirty-six-block business district in northern Tulsa lay smoldering; a model community destroyed and a major African-American economic movement resoundingly defused.

That night's carnage left over 3,000 African-Americans dead out of the 15,000 population and encompassed over 600 successful businesses lost in thirty-six square blocks. Among these were twenty-one churches, twenty-one restaurant, thirty grocery stores, and two movie theaters, plus a hospital, a bank, a post office, libraries, schools, law offices, a half dozen private airplanes, and even a bus system. When the average student went to school on Black Wall Street, he wore a suit and tie because of the morals and respect they were taught at a young age. The mainstay of the community was to educate every child. Nepotism was the one word they believed in, and that's what we need to take your wealth with you; so why not build another Black Wall Street?

Reference: http://www.blackwallstreet.freeservers. com/ The Black Holocaust Society; Greenwood Cultural Center: http://www.greenwood cultural center.com; The Tulsa Race Riot of 1921 by I. Marc Carlson: http://tul-saraceriot. Word Press. command and http://www.ebony. com/ black-history/the-destruction-of-black-wall-street- 405#axzz4QEDfpXDy)

(d.)   "Christianity and the Negro Race"

I believe the Bible to be the "Basic Instructions Before Living Eternally;" if the dominants would realize and practice it to its fullest, then we can eliminate most of what's been written by man, and politics would work in a way that is fair for all mankind. Politics is not a bad word, but Webster's dictionary said it is used in our society as shrewdness in managing, contriving, or dealing; sagacious in promoting a policy; shrewdly tactful. Well, that makes it bad, because it goes against the true public transcript, which is the Bible. But remember, God has laws and some men turn them into policies for everyone to follow. Therefore, I suggest that maybe all that mankind has written was started as a rumor and then it became a Public Transcript. A good example of a Hidden Transcript is in the name of Religion and Politics against a certain race of people, most of whom to this day still don't realize why they are of a certain denomination. On the other hand, it was a Public Transcript of the Religious Elites who happen to be of another certain race of people (White).

I wrote this essay, "Christianity and the Negro Race," between 2000 & 2001 and the only thing that may have changed since that time is that the title would be different; instead of Negro Race it would read Black Race/African Americans. Edward Wilmot Blyden wrote "Christianity, Islam and the Negro Race." He was from the Virgin Islands and lived from 1832 to 1912. I find it remarkable that Black people during that time period were discerning the wrong doings of the Whites/Elites who used Christianity for their social and political gain and then put it on paper. When I read this article, I was amazed at the history that I found, so I analyzed that information as a Spiritual Holocaust and The Mark of the Beast.

I viewed it as a "Spiritual Holocaust" for both parties involved because the Africans/Blacks' soul and spirit were being cut off from God the Creator by the White Elites, and for the White Elites their soul and spirit were heading straight for Hell (The Lake of Fire) for their wrong doings. The Mark of the Beast part is played out by the Whites/Elites, because of the false usage of Christianity to gain their Social (Education), Political, and Economic power in this country. They physically enslaved Black people, and mentally misled the under privileged White people who were unable to read, like most of the Black people who it was against the law. Reading and Education are still the keys to freedom, because if a person can read and comprehend what they have read, then it will be hard for them to be misled. In this country and others alike, when someone speaks about the Holocaust, it is quickly thought to be about what the Nazis did to the Jews during World War II. Well, I'm here to tell you that what the Whites/Elites did to the Africans/Black people was and still is far worse than what the Nazis did to the Jews.

The American Elites don't want history told as it should be told, because there were more than six million Africans/Black people slaughtered during the period of taking these people from their natural habitat. The Bible speaks about two Beasts in the Book of Revelation starting in chapter six, one being Political and the other Religious. Well, in that story I see both being manifested to their fullest potential. The White Elites in both of these arenas used everything at their disposal to make sure that the Bible was interpreted as though they were operating within the parameters of the Word of God. This was done especially in the South, because the Negroes and the average White person who received the Gospel of Christ received it in a travestied and diluted version. the Black person it was to keep them in bondage physically and mentally, and for the average White person it was to uplift them so they could see themselves better than the Negro/Black people.

The White Elites used and still uses Christianity as one of their major blinders in this nation; they had each party involved thinking of themselves as one being superior and the other being inferior to the other as a check and balance within the social and political arena. This superiority and inferiority complex game is still played today, and as long as White people feel they are superior to any Black person or Person of Color regardless of his or her accomplishments, they are still operating under that influence of the Two Beasts. The average White person cannot see that they have been used by a system of wickedness, and the White Elites cannot see past their riches that the Two Beasts have used them to blind others from the Truth. The old saying is What comes around, goes around, for there is an appointed time for all things in the natural to be judged by what is Spiritual and True, for that which is not True will be Consumed by Fire. Christianity has gotten a bad rap because of the misuse of it; Christianity is not a Religion, but it's a Reality of Life and for the African/Black/Negro and People of Color, the reality has been what the Word of God has said it to be.

I thank God that in this day and time reading is not illegal, because if it were, the African/Black/Negro and People of Color "Americans" would be in the same position as they were in about thirty years ago. The only thing that's holding people back in Christianity is the Tradition of Men being taught, and not enough of what the Bible has really said to mankind. I hope that the release of the shackles of Spiritual Holocaust and The Mark of the Beast someday be Blotted Out of your mind; therefore, pray to God for His Holy Spirit to Circumcise Your Heart and Mind so His Love can enter your life. Repent of your sins and accept His only begotten Son Jesus Christ as your Lord and Savior. Once you have done that, get a revelation behind the meaning of Ephesians 6:12 (KJV) "We wrestle not against flesh and blood, but against principalities, against power, against the rulers of the darkness of this world, against spiritual wickedness in high places."

Satan is the Prince of this world, but Jesus is the King of kings and Lord of lords, so if you are a child of the King, you have all Rights to the Inheritances that He has left for all His Children that NO man or Satan can take away unless we let him to-do-so. Satan has been defeated, and he only wants to take as many Souls to the "Lake of Fire" with him: Satan is - the only one by name who has been sentence to death: Ezekiel 28: 13-29 (KJV) says "Thou hast been in Eden the garden of God; every precious stone was thy covering, the sardius, topaz, and the diamond, the beryl, the onyx, and the jasper, the sapphire, the emerald, and the carbuncle, and gold: the workmanship of thy tabrets and of thy pipes was prepared in thee in the day that thou wast created. [14] Thou art the anointed cherub that covereth; and I have set thee so: thou wast upon the holy mountain of God; thou hast walked up and down in the midst of the stones of fire. [15] Thou wast perfect in thy ways from the day that thou wast created, till iniquity was found in thee. [16] By the multitude of thy merchandise they have filled the midst of thee with violence, and thou hast sinned: therefore I will cast thee as profane out of the mountain of God: and I will destroy thee, O covering cherub, from the midst of the stones of fire. [17] Thine heart was lifted up because of thy beauty, thou hast corrupted thy wisdom by reason of thy brightness: I will cast thee to the ground, I will lay thee before kings, that they may behold thee. [18] Thou hast defiled thy sanctuaries by the multitude of thine iniquities, by the iniquity of thy traffick; therefore will I bring forth a fire from the midst of thee, it shall devour thee, and I will bring thee to ashes upon the earth in the sight of all them that behold thee. [19] All they that know thee among the people shall be astonished at thee: thou shalt be a terror, and never shalt thou be any more."

God has written you and I a letter call the BIBLE for your spiritual edification of winning the war while in the flesh. A reminder to all people from Colossians 3:25 (KJV) says "But he that doeth wrong shall receive for the wrong which he hath done and there is no respect of persons." If the White/Elites do not Repent for their wrong doings, for what they have done and are doing to Black People and People-of-Color, payday is coming as stated in Roman 12:19 (KJV) "Vengeance is mine; I repay, saith the Lord."

I must reiterate that the "Subjects" I have used in the "Practicality of the Four Horns" were in no way to be Racial or about Race, I am a Black Man that write from my experiences, education, and socioeconomic background that forms my perspectives. As people grow older the "Perspectives" and "Prospective" of history has a way of repeating itself; therefore, knowing "there is nothing new under the sun" just want to remind and educate the reader who has never heard what I am writing about; especially pertaining to the "Practicality of the Four Horns". For those who do not believe what is in this book, I would say you have been conditioned to the "Power of the Pin" advocated by the Elites/White men. Regardless of your Ethnicity, Race, Religion or Socioeconomic status, if you are a Believer in God (The Father, Son & Holy Spirit) Satan is your Enemy. Therefore, Be Watchmen & Watchwomen because the Lords' Day is at hand!

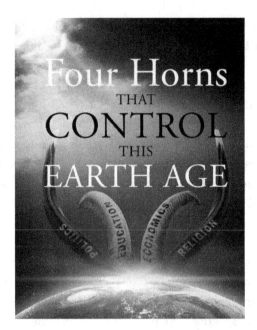

Remember: Job 1:8 (KJV) *says* "Then the LORD said to Satan, have you considered my servant Job? There is no one on earth like him; he is blameless and upright, a man who fears God and shuns evil."

Can God ask this question and make that same statement to Satan about You as he did about Job?

CHAPTER 3

JESUS'S IMPORTANT TEACHINGS

"The Beatitudes,"
"The 8 Woes"
"The End Time of this Earth Age" (Sealing the Mind)

"The Beatitudes"
Matthew 5: 3-12 (KJV)

"The Beatitudes" come from the opening verses of the famous *Sermon on the Mount* delivered by Jesus recorded in *Matthew 5:3-12 (KJV)*. Here Jesus stated several blessings, each beginning with the phrase, **"Blessed are ..."** ... The word *beatitude* comes from the Latin word *beatitudo*, meaning *blessedness*. The word "Blessed" means "Happy" and the *Beatitude* are at the core of Christ's teaching, they fulfill the promise made to the Jewish people by pointing beyond earthly happiness to the eternal happiness of heaven.

Matthew 5: 1-12 (KJV) "¹And seeing the multitudes, he went up into a mountain: and when he was set, his disciples came unto him:²And Jesus opened his mouth and taught them, saying:"

³ *"Blessed are the poor in spirit, for theirs is the kingdom of heaven."*

⁴ *"Blessed are those who mourn, for they shall be comforted."*

⁵ *"Blessed are the meek, for they shall inherit the earth."*

⁶ *"Blessed are those who hunger and thirst for righteousness, for they shall be satisfied."*

⁷ *"Blessed are the merciful, for they shall receive mercy."*

⁸ *"Blessed are the pure in heart, for they shall see God."*

⁹ *"Blessed are the peacemakers, for they shall be called sons of God."*

¹⁰ *"Blessed are those who are persecuted for righteousness' sake, for theirs is the kingdom of heaven."*

¹¹ *"Blessed are you when others revile you and persecute you and utter all kinds of evil against you falsely on my account. Rejoice and be glad, for your reward is great in heaven, for so they persecuted the prophets who were before you."*

Therefore, the reward promised in each **Beatitude** is primarily heaven and most importantly I believe is that they reveal the goal of human existence and the ultimate purpose of human acts. God calls us to His own **Beatitude,** because the vocation is addressed to everyone personally, but also to the Church that has to accept the promises and live from it by faith. Therefore, if we live according to the plan of Christ we shall have a foretaste of the "happiness" of heaven in this life

"The Eight Woes"
Matthew 23: 13, 14, 15, 16, 23, 25, 27, and 29 (KJV)

The 23ʳᵈ chapter of Matthew is often called *"the Chapter of the 8 Woes."* Jesus pronounced these *"Woes" upon the religious scribes and Pharisees, and they are found in verses 13, 14, 15, 16, 23, 25, 27, and 29.*

¹³ *"But woe unto you, scribes and Pharisees, hypocrites! for ye shut up the kingdom of heaven against men: for ye neither go in yourselves, neither suffer ye them that are entering to go in."*

¹⁴ *"Woe unto you, scribes and Pharisees, hypocrites! for ye devour widows' houses, and for a pretence make long prayer: therefore ye shall receive the greater damnation."*

¹⁵ *"Woe unto you, scribes and Pharisees, hypocrites! for ye compass sea and land to make one proselyte, and when he is made, ye make him twofold more the child of hell than yourselves."*

¹⁶ *"Woe unto you, ye blind guides, which say, Whosoever shall swear by the temple, it is nothing; but whosoever shall swear by the gold of the temple, he is a debtor!"*

²³ *"Woe unto you, scribes and Pharisees, hypocrites! for ye pay tithe of mint and anise and cummin, and have omitted the weightier matters of the law, judgment, mercy, and faith: these ought ye to have done, and not to leave the other undone."*

²⁵ *"Woe unto you, scribes and Pharisees, hypocrites! for ye make clean the outside of the cup and of the platter, but within they are full of extortion and excess."*

²⁷ *"Woe unto you, scribes and Pharisees, hypocrites! for ye are like unto whited sepulchres, which indeed appear beautiful outward, but are within full of dead men's bones, and of all uncleanness."*

²⁹ *"Woe unto you, scribes and Pharisees, hypocrites! because ye build the tombs of the prophets, and garnish the sepulchres of the righteous,"*

Seven times Jesus said, **"Woe unto you, scribes and Pharisees, hypocrites!"** There was such a deceptive spirit upon the *scribes and Pharisees* that they were not even aware they were hypocrites and blind guides. They thought they were serving God, and that it was Jesus who was deceived and motivated by the devil Matthew 12:24 (KJV). They had become so deceived they were unable to know the truth. They were the religious leaders of that day and thought they were leading the people according to the will of God. *Do you believe there are scribes and Pharisees today—religious leaders with the same characteristics as the scribes and Pharisees in the Bible? Do you think real Christians can become deceived scribes and Pharisees? They are more dangerous than those who are openly opposed to Christianity. They are more dangerous because they appear righteous, and many people are deceived by them.*

The fact that Jesus pronounced eight woes is significant. <u>Seven spiritually is the number of completeness and eight is a number of a new order.</u> For example, seven days complete one week but the eighth day begins a new order. The number eight in Scripture can refer to a person of a new order either in a good or bad sense. <u>Christians pass through many stages before being in the likeness and image of the Lord. Christians, in general, are like the tree of knowledge of good and evil and the process of the Christ nature has begun in them,</u> <u>but still have the sinful Adamic nature of their flesh life</u>. If they continue to partake of the divine nature II Peter 1:4 (KJV), their *sinful nature will be overcome by the divine life of the Lord coming forth in them. Thus, they become a new order, sons of God—old things have passed away and all things have become new* II Corinthians 5:17 (KJV) and <u>*this is what all Christians should be striving for daily.*</u>

The same thing can happen in a negative sense. People can become a new order by taking on the satanic nature. Jesus calls them tares, sons of the wicked one, in Matthew chapter thirteen. So, Jesus pronouncing eight woes upon the scribes and Pharisees declared them a satanic new order. In Revelation 12:9 (KJV) the Satan - *devil* is called a *serpent*—the role he was in when in the Garden of Eden in Genesis; Jesus after pronouncing the eight *"Woes"* upon the scribes and Pharisees, He said to them, in Matthew 23:33 (KJV) ***"Ye serpents, ye generation of vipers, how can ye escape the damnation of hell?"*** In Matthew 23:36 (KJV) Jesus states ***"Verily I say unto you, All these things shall come upon this generation."*** The scribes and Pharisees were not a religious group apart from the Jewish religion; they were the very core of it. They were considered the *religious elite*, those who led the people in the ways of God. In like manner the scribes and Pharisees of today are in the midst of Christianity. They are found among the leaders of Christianity and that is Satan's way of trying to defeat and destroy the Kingdom of God. He will not be successful, but in his efforts, he will deceive (and has deceived) many Christians. Because of this the Lord says, *"All these things shall come unto this generation."* The judgments of God will come upon this generation through the *"Woes"* Jesus prophesied upon the scribes and Pharisees. The woes Jesus pronounced became the channel for the judgments of God to come upon the characteristics of the scribes and Pharisees of every age. When Jesus spoke, He spoke a living Word John 6:63 (KJV). That means His words are as living and active today as they were at the time, because He spoke them. So, not only will the scribes and Pharisees of that day not be able to escape the damnation of hell, but all who have that same nature in this day won't be able to escape the damnation of hell, either.

NOTE: Read for yourself, pray and ask God for Spiritual Discernment; then your eyes the gateway to your mind will be enlighten of those whom you have put as your Pastor or whatever you call the leader of the Church you attend.

Definition of Woe

1: A condition of deep suffering from misfortune, affliction, or grief
2: ruinous trouble: calamity, affliction economic woes

Definition of Calamity

1: a disastrous event marked by great loss and lasting distress and suffering calamities of nature an economic calamity.
2: a state of deep distress or misery caused by major misfortune or loss

Definition of Affliction

1: a cause of persistent pain or distress a mysterious affliction
2: great suffering felt empathy with their affliction

3: the state of being afflicted by something that causes suffering her affliction with polio. Seven times Jesus said, in Matthew 23:1-12 (KJV) "Then spake Jesus to the multitude, and to his disciples, ²Saying, "The scribes and the Pharisees sit in Moses' seat: ³All therefore whatsoever they bid you observe, that observe and do; but do not ye after their works: for they say and do not. ⁴For they bind heavy burdens and grievous to be borne, and lay them on men's shoulders; but they themselves will not move them with one of their fingers. ⁵But all their works they do for to be seen of men: they make broad their phylacteries, and enlarge the borders of their garments,⁶And love the uppermost rooms at feasts, and the chief seats in the synagogues, ⁷And greetings in the markets, and to be called of men, Rabbi, Rabbi. ⁸But be not ye called Rabbi: for one is your Master, even Christ; and all ye are brethren. ⁹And call no man your father upon the earth: for one is your Father, which is in heaven. ¹⁰Neither be ye called masters: for one is your Master, even Christ. ¹¹But he that is greatest among you shall be your servant. ¹²And whosoever shall exalt himself shall be abased; and he that shall humble himself shall be exalted

Note

Jesus's Message because of the Eight Woes: Matthew 23: 31-36 (KJV) says "Wherefore ye be witnesses unto yourselves, that ye are the children of them which killed the prophets. ³²Fill ye up then the measure of your fathers. ³³Ye serpents, ye generation of vipers, how can ye escape the damnation of hell? ³⁴Wherefore, behold, I send unto you prophets, and wise men, and scribes: and some of them ye shall kill and crucify; and some of them shall ye scourge in your synagogues, and persecute them from city to city: ³⁵That upon you may come all the righteous blood shed upon the earth, from the blood of righteous Abel unto the blood of Zacharias son of Barachias, whom ye slew between the temple and the altar. ³⁶Verily I say unto you, All these things shall come upon this generation."

Note

Now that I have given you a foretaste of Jesus's teaching and before going forward, I believe this is a good place to reiterate on some very important *truths* and something that I wrote in my first book *"Spiritually Circumcise Your Heart and Mind."*

In the beginning was the Word, and the Word was with God, and the Word was God. John 1:1 (KJV) In addition, "In the Beginning God created the Heaven (s) and Earth." Genesis 1:1 (KJV) Never said when the beginning was and no one knows, but by scientific knowledge the Earth is billions of years old and God did not create anything *"void and without form"* as stated in Genesis 1:2 (KJV), because ***God (YHVH) created all things for His pleasure.***

Proof

Isaiah 45:18 (KJV) says "For thus saith the Lord that created the heavens; God himself that formed the Earth and made it; he hath established it, he created it not in "Vain," he formed it to be "Inhabited:" I am the Lord; and there is none else."

Proof

Jeremiah 4:22-27 (KJV) says "For my people is foolish, they have not known me; they are sottish (meaning stupid) children, and they none understanding: they are wise to do evil, but to do good they have no knowledge. 23I beheld the earth, and lo, it was without form, void; and the heavens, and they had no light. {Reference in Isaiah 24:19 (KJV) and Genesis 1:2 (KJV)} 24I beheld the mountains, and, lo, they tremble, and all the hills moved lightly. 25I beheld, and, lo, there was no man, and all the birds of the heavens were fled. 26I beheld, and, lo, the fruitful place was a wilderness, and all the cities thereof were broken down at the presence of the Lord, and by his fierce anger. 27For thus hath the Lord said, The whole land shall be desolate; yet will I not make a full end."

Note

Out of God's fierce anger He shook the Earth possibly by natural means (meteorites, earthquakes, and or volcanoes) in doing so the Earth now has two Norths (The Magnetic North & True North).

Proof

Hebrews 12: 26 (KJV) says "Whose voice then shook the earth: but now he hath promised, saying, Yet once more I shake not the earth only, but also heaven." All of that was written so one must rightly divide God's Word because in Genesis 1:2 (KJV) the word (Was) is (hayah) and in the Hebrew language that means "Became" and that gives that verse a different meaning and prospective. With that being explained one should ask themselves why did the Earth Become Without Form and Void (tohuw va bohuw) that means a Vain, empty, wicked and a confused wilderness. The Earth became void and that (darkness) (besides being literally dark) was not it (Lucifer) who became Satan, which caused such confusion then and still does today to the uncircumcised Hearts and Minds!

READ: Isaiah 14: 12-17 (KJV) and Ezekiel 28 (KJV) they both describe Lucifer's Fall. In the New Testament when Jesus and others say the phase, "since the Foundation of the World," Jesus and others are talking about the (Katabole) meaning the (Casting Down). Foundation is (Katabole) #2602 in the "Strong's Exhausted Concordance" Greek section. Remember I said rightly divide the Word, in Genesis 1: 2-25 (KJV) all those verses begin with (And) which is a (Polysyndeton) that denotes something with Great Emphasis is About to Happen or is Happening. The last part of Genesis1:2 (KJV) "And the Spirit of God moved upon the face of the waters," at that moment this (Dispensation of Time) and the (Plan of Salvation) began.

Note

II Peter 3: 5-7 (KJV) says "For this they willingly are ignorant of, that by the Word of God the heavens were of old, and the earth standing out of the water and in the water. ⁶Whereby the world that then was, being overflowed with water, perished: ⁷But the heavens and the earth which are now, by the same word are kept in store, reserved unto fire against the say of judgement and perdition of ungodly men."

"The End Time of this Earth Age" (Sealing the Mind)
References (KJV): Matthew 24, Mark 13, Luke 21, Revelation 6, Ezekiel 40-44, Daniel 7: 23 Daniel 8: 20-26, Daniel 9: 25 and Daniel 11: 21-24.

In this chapter "The End Time of this Earth Age" (Sealing the Mind) when using different verses from one of the three synoptic gospels (Matthew, Mark and Luke, because they include many of the same stories, often in a similar sequence and or sometimes identical wording); I will indicate which Gospel is being used. I will mix them together to become one story, because I believe the verses I use gives more emphasis of what Jesus was telling His Disciples that includes us as His followers should lookout for and prepare ourselves for when that "Time" comes we can endure until the end.

Note

Jesus makes Daniel relevant, therefore I tell you when Jesus says, "I have foretold you all things," He is mainly talking about that which is in the (Old Testament) of the Bible.

Note

The Gospels are part of the "Old Testament" and the (New Testament) starts in Acts; think about it, for a (Testament) to be legal the person Jesus (The Word in the Flesh) must have too been dead/died. Hum, you may say to yourself, when was Jesus here in the (Old Testament) and I tell you He was as Melchizedek (who had no father or mother)!!

Matthew 24: 1-9 (KJV) says "And Jesus went out and departed from the temple: and his disciples came to him for to shew him the buildings of the temple. ²And Jesus said unto them, See ye not all these things? verily I say unto you, There shall not be left here one stone upon another, that shall not be thrown down. ³ And as he sat upon the mount of Olives, the disciples came unto him privately, saying, Tell us, when shall these things be? and what shall be the sign of thy coming, and of the end of the world? ⁴ And Jesus answered and said unto them, Take heed that no man deceive you. ⁵ For many shall come in my name, saying, I am Christ; and shall deceive many. ⁶ And ye shall hear of wars and rumours of wars: see that ye be not troubled: for all these things must come to pass, but the end is not yet. ⁷ For nation shall rise against nation, and kingdom against kingdom: and there shall be famines, and pestilences, and earthquakes, in divers' places. ⁸ All these are the beginning of sorrows. ⁹ Then shall they deliver you up to be afflicted, and shall <u>kill you</u>: and ye shall be hated of all nations for my name's sake."

Mark13: 9-15 (KJV) says "But take heed to yourselves: for they shall deliver you up to councils; and in the synagogues ye <u>shall be beaten</u>: and ye shall be brought before rulers and kings for my sake, for a testimony against them. ¹⁰ And the gospel must first be published among all nations. ¹¹ But when they shall lead you, and deliver you up, take no thought beforehand what ye shall speak, neither do ye premeditate: but whatsoever shall be given you in that hour, that speak ye: for it is not ye that speak, but the Holy Ghost. ¹² Now the brother shall betray the brother to death, and the father the son; and children shall rise up against their parents, and shall cause them to be put to death. (NOTE: "shall betray the brother to death," this death is Satan. Think about it, Satan is coming as Jesus and Jesus would not "Kill" you, He is the Savior!) ¹³ And ye shall be hated of all men for my name's sake: but he that shall endure unto the end, the same shall be saved. ¹⁴ But when ye shall see the abomination of desolation, spoken of by Daniel the prophet, standing where it ought not, (let him that readeth understand,) then let them that be in Judaea flee to the mountains: ¹⁵ And let him that is on the housetop not go down into the house, neither enter therein, to take anything out of his house:"

Luke 21: 18-24 (KJV) says "But there shall not an hair of your head perish. ¹⁹ In your patience possess ye your souls. ²⁰ And when ye shall see Jerusalem compassed with armies, then know that the desolation thereof is nigh. ²¹

Then let them that are in Judea flee to the mountains; and let them which are in the midst of it depart out; and let not them that are in the countries enter thereinto [22] For these be the days of vengeance, that all things which are written may be fulfilled. [23] But woe unto them that are with child, and to them that give suck, in those days! for there shall be great distress in the land, and wrath upon this people. [24] And they shall fall by the edge of the sword, and shall be led away captive into all nations: and Jerusalem shall be trodden down of the Gentiles, until the times of the Gentiles be fulfilled."

Mark13:19-23 (KJV) says "For in those days shall be affliction, such as was not from the beginning of the creation which God created unto this time, neither shall be. [20] And except that the Lord had shortened those days, no flesh should be saved: but for the elect's sake, whom he hath chosen, he hath shortened the days. [21] And then if any man shall say to you, Lo, here is Christ; or, lo, he is there; believe him not: [22] For false Christs and false prophets shall rise, and shall shew signs and wonders, to seduce, if it were possible, even the elect. [23] But take ye heed: behold, I have foretold you all things."

{Satan's Tribulation/First Tribulation/Pre-Tribulation will only last Five Months, not the original Seven Years as written in the Old Testament} Revelation 9: 1-6 (KJV) says "And the fifth angel sounded, and I saw a star fall from heaven unto the earth: and to him was given the key of the bottomless pit. [2] And he opened the bottomless pit; and there arose a smoke out of the pit, as the smoke of a great furnace; and the sun and the air were darkened by reason of the smoke of the pit. [3] And there came out of the smoke locusts upon the earth: and unto them was given power, as the scorpions of the earth have power. [4] And it was commanded them that they should not hurt the grass of the earth, neither any green thing, neither any tree; but only those men which have not the seal of God in their foreheads. [5] And to them it was given that they should not kill them, but that they should be tormented five months: and their torment was as the torment of a scorpion, when he striketh a man. [6] And in those days shall men seek death, and shall not find it; and shall desire to die, and death shall flee from them."

Note

That "star" in verse one is Satan, and he knows he only has a short time to do his thing before Jesus returns and the millennium begins.

Luke 21:25-36 (KJV) says "And there shall be signs in the sun, and in the moon, and in the stars; and upon the earth distress of nations, with perplexity; the sea and the waves roaring; [26] Men's hearts failing them for fear, and for looking after those things which are coming on the earth: for the powers of heaven shall be shaken. [27] And then shall they see the Son of man coming in a cloud with power and great glory. [28] And when these things begin to come to pass, then look up, and lift up your heads; for your redemption draweth nigh. [29] And he spake to them a parable; Behold the fig tree, and all the trees; [30] When they now shoot forth, ye see and know of your own selves that summer is now nigh at hand. [31] So likewise ye, when ye see these things come to pass, know ye that the kingdom of God is nigh at hand. [32] Verily I say unto you, This generation shall not pass away, till all be fulfilled. [33] Heaven and earth shall pass away: but my words shall not pass away. [34] And take heed to yourselves, lest at any time your hearts be overcharged with surfeiting, and drunkenness, and cares of this life, and so that day come upon you unawares. [35] For as a snare shall it come on all them that dwell on the face of the whole earth. [36] Watch ye therefore, and pray always, that ye may be accounted worthy to escape all these things that shall come to pass, and to stand before the Son of man."

Mark13:24-37 (KJV) says "But in those days, after that tribulation, the sun shall be darkened, and the moon shall not give her light, [25] And the stars of heaven shall fall, and the powers that are in heaven shall be shaken. [26] And then shall they see the Son of man coming in the clouds with great power and glory. [27] And then shall he send his angels, and shall gather together his elect from the four winds, from the uttermost part of the earth to the uttermost part of heaven. [28] Now learn a parable of the fig tree; When her branch is yet tender, and putteth forth leaves, ye know that summer is near: [29] So ye in like manner, when ye shall see these things come to pass, know that it is nigh, even at the doors. [30] Verily I say unto you, that this generation shall not pass, till all these things be done. [31] Heaven and earth shall pass away: but my words shall not pass away. ³² But of that day and that hour knoweth no man, no, not the angels which are in heaven, neither the Son, but the Father. ³³ Take ye heed, watch and pray: for ye know not when the time is. ³⁴ For the Son of Man is as a man taking a far journey, who left his house, and gave authority to his servants, and to every man his work, and commanded the porter to watch. ³⁵ Watch ye therefore: for ye know not when the master of the house cometh, at even, or at midnight, or at the cockcrowing, or in the morning: ³⁶ Lest coming suddenly he find you sleeping. ³⁷ And what I say unto you I say unto all, Watch."

Matthew 24:10-51 (KJV) says "And then shall many be offended, and shall betray one another, and shall hate one another. ¹¹ And many false prophets shall rise and shall deceive many. ¹² And because iniquity shall abound, the love of many shall wax cold. ¹³ But he that shall endure unto the end, the same shall be saved. ¹⁴ And this gospel of the kingdom shall be preached in all the world for a witness unto all nations; and then shall the end come. ¹⁵ When ye therefore shall see the abomination of desolation, spoken of by Daniel the prophet, stand in the holy place, (whoso readeth, let him understand): ¹⁶ Then let them which be in Judaea flee into the mountains: ¹⁷ Let him which is on the housetop not come down to take anything out of his house: ¹⁸ Neither let him which is in the field return back to take his clothes. ¹⁹ And woe unto them that are with child, and to them that give suck in those days! ²⁰ But pray ye that your flight be not in the winter, neither on the sabbath day: ²¹ For then shall be great tribulation, such as was not since the beginning of the world to this time, no, nor ever shall be. ²² And except those days should be shortened, there should no flesh be saved: but for the elect's sake those days shall be shortened. ²³ Then if any man shall say unto you, Lo, here is Christ, or there; believe it not. ²⁴ For there shall arise false Christs, and false prophets, and shall shew great signs and wonders; insomuch that, if it were possible, they shall deceive the very elect. ²⁵ Behold, I have told you before. ²⁶ Wherefore if they shall say unto you, Behold, he is in the desert; go not forth: behold, he is in the secret chambers; believe it not. ²⁷ For as the lightning cometh out of the east, and shineth even unto the west; so shall also the coming of the Son of man be. ²⁸ For wheresoever the carcase is, there will the eagles be gathered together. ²⁹ Immediately after the tribulation of those days shall the sun be darkened, and the moon shall not give her light, and the stars shall fall from heaven, and the powers of the heavens shall be shaken: [30] And then shall appear the sign of the Son of man in heaven: and then shall all the tribes of the earth mourn, and they shall see the Son of man coming in the clouds of heaven with power and great glory. [31] And he shall send his angels with a great sound of a trumpet, and they shall gather together his elect from the four winds, from one end of heaven to the other. [32] Now learn a parable of the fig tree; When his branch is yet tender, and putteth forth leaves, ye know that summer is nigh: [33] So likewise ye, when ye shall see all these things, know that it is near, even at the doors. [34] Verily I say unto you, This generation shall not pass, till all these things be fulfilled. [35] Heaven and earth shall pass away, but my words shall not pass away. [36] But of that day and hour knoweth no man, no, not the angels of heaven, but my Father only. [37] But as the days of Noe were, so shall also the coming of the Son of man be. [38] For as in the days that were before the flood they were eating and drinking, marrying and giving in marriage, until the day that Noe entered into the ark, [39] And knew not until the flood came, and took them all away; so shall also the coming of the Son of man be. [40] Then shall two be in the field; the one shall be taken, and the other left. [41] Two women shall be grinding at the mill; the one shall be taken, and the other left. [42] Watch therefore: for ye know not what hour your Lord doth come. [43] But know this, that if the goodman of the house had known in what watch the thief would come, he would have watched, and would not have suffered his house to be broken up. [44] Therefore be ye also ready: for in such an hour as ye think not the Son of man cometh. [45] Who then is a faithful and wise servant, whom his lord hath made ruler over his household, to give them meat in due season? [46] Blessed is that servant, whom his lord when he cometh shall find so doing. [47] Verily I say unto you, That he shall make him ruler over all his goods. [48] But and if that evil servant shall say in his heart, My lord delayeth his coming; [49] And shall begin to smite his fellow servants, and to eat and drink with the drunken; 50 The lord of that servant shall come in a day when he looketh not for him, and in an hour that he is not aware of, [51] And shall cut him asunder, and appoint him his portion with the hypocrites: there shall be weeping and gnashing of teeth."

Note

These are other scriptures that are prophecies of *"The End Times"* and Prophecies are being fulfilled daily.

Daniel 7:23 (KJV) says "Thus he said, The *fourth beast* shall be the fourth kingdom upon earth, which shall be diverse from all kingdoms, and shall devour the whole earth, and shall tread it down, and break it in pieces."

Daniel 8: 23-26 (KJV) says "And in the latter time of their kingdom, When the transgressors have reached their fullness, A king shall arise, Having fierce features, Who understands sinister schemes. [24]His power shall be mighty, but not by his own power; He shall destroy fearfully, And shall prosper and thrive; He shall destroy the mighty, and also the holy people. [25] Through his cunning He shall cause deceit to prosper under his rule; And he shall exalt himself in his heart. He shall destroy many in their prosperity. He shall even rise against the Prince of princes; But he shall be broken without human means. [26]And the vision of the evenings and mornings Which was told is true; Therefore seal up the vision, For it refers to many days in the future."

Daniel 9:25 (KJV) says "Then he shall confirm a covenant with many for one week; But in the middle of the week He shall bring an end to sacrifice and offering. And on the wing of abominations shall be one who makes desolate, Even until the consummation, which is determined, Is poured out on the desolate."

Daniel 11: 21-24 (KJV) says "And in his estate shall stand up a vile person, to whom they shall not give the honour of the kingdom: but he shall come in peaceably, and obtain the kingdom by flatteries. [22] And with the arms of a flood shall they be overflown from before him, and shall be broken; yea, also the prince of the covenant.[23]And after the league made with him, he shall work deceitfully: for he shall come up, and shall become strong with a small people. [24]He shall enter peaceably even upon the fattest places of the province; and he shall do that which his fathers have not done, nor his fathers' fathers; he shall scatter among them the prey, and spoil, and riches: yea, and he shall forecast his devices against the strong holds, even for a time. ²⁵And he shall stir up his power and his courage against the king of the south with a great army; and the king of the south shall be stirred up to battle with a very great and mighty army; but he shall not stand for they shall forecast devices against him."

Summary

In Chapter 1 of my first book *"Spiritually Circumcise Your Heart & Mind"* I continue to explain the rest of Genesis chapters 1, 2, and 3; my advice is carefully read these chapters over and over and Pray that the Holy Spirit can talk to your Heart and Mind that Truth can be revealed and resonate in your soul and spirit before continuing reading the rest of the book. The main reason for writing that book is because there are too many Traditions of Men being Preached and Taught right from the Pulpit today. Jesus gave The Great Commission, go Preach and Teach All Over the World, because I have told you everything. Knowing that there is going to be a Great Apostasy coming and what is being taught just adds on for MANY to be deceived.

My suggestion is to get a clear understanding of what Jesus said in Matthew 24 (KJV), Mark 13 (KJV), and Luke 21 (KJV). Jesus gives everyone the *Seven Seals* that will sustain their Salvation and not be in Satan's camp, because Jesus wants a Virgin Bride for the wedding. In Revaluations John was in the Spirit to receive what would come about and was given the (7 Seals, 7 Trumps and 7 Vails). In addition, Jesus told John which churches He was pleased with; out of the seven churches there was only 2 that met His approval (Smyrna and Philadelphia). If the church you are attend does not Peach and Teach what Smyrna and Philadelphia did, and you don not study for yourself to show yourself approved before God; then the Great Apostasy will overtake you. Reason being is because you will be pregnant with Satan's lies and therefore, worshipping "The Anti-Christ." That's why Jesus states "Woe to those are with child when He returns" this is spiritual in nature, because it is a blessing for those who can bear children. Many believe that Jesus is going to Rapture them and the church away from Satan and his turmoil that will be going on in the world when God pours out His Raft on all the Rudiments of Evilness on the earth. Number one thing is that Rapture is not in the Bible and Jesus is not going to FLY anyone away. Therefore, Christians are always to have the

Gospel Armour on, because there are no *jet packs* mentioned in that Armour of God. Jesus gave Christians Power over All their enemies; therefore, Stand in Faith for Jesus is with you.

Good Example: *The Fiery Furnace in Daniel 3:20-25 (KJV)* says "And he commanded certain mighty men of valor who *were* in his army to bind Shadrach, Meshach, and Abed-Nego, and cast them into the burning fiery furnace. ²¹ Then these men were bound in their coats, their trousers, their turbans, and their other garments, and were cast into the midst of the burning fiery furnace. ²² Therefore, because the king's command was urgent, and the furnace exceedingly hot, the flame of the fire killed those men who took up Shadrach, Meshach, and Abed-Nego. ²³ And these three men, Shadrach, Meshach, and Abed-Nego, fell down bound into the midst of the burning fiery furnace. ²⁴ Then King Nebuchadnezzar was astonished; and he rose in haste and spoke, saying to his counselors, Did we not cast three men bound into the midst of the fire? They answered and said to the king, "True, O king." ²⁵ "Look!" he answered, "I see four men loose, walking in the midst of the fire; and they are not hurt, and the form of the fourth is like the Son of God."

<u>Another Good Example:</u> *The Lion's Den* in *Daniel 6: 24-27 (KJV)* says "And the king gave the command, and they brought those men who had accused Daniel, and they cast them into the den of lions—them, their children, and their wives; and the lions overpowered them, and broke all their bones in pieces before they ever came to the bottom of the den. ²⁵ Then King Darius wrote: To all peoples, nations, and languages that dwell in all the earth: Peace be multiplied to you. ²⁶ I make a decree that in every dominion of my kingdom men must tremble and fear before the God of Daniel. For He *is* the living God, And steadfast forever; His kingdom is the one which shall not be destroyed, And His dominion shall endure to the end. ²⁷ He delivers and rescues, And He works signs and wonders In heaven and on earth, Who has delivered Daniel from the power of the lions."

> *God is no Respecter of Person and knows who*
> *to Save and whom to let be Destroyed!*

CHAPTER 4

THE GREAT APOSTASY &
SPIRIT OF SLUMBER

References (KJV): **Great Apostasy** (II Chronicles 15: 1-15) and (Deuteronomy 13: 1-18); *Jesus* (Matthew 24: 3-24, Luke 8:11-15 and John 6:63-70); *Apostle Paul* (Galatians 1: 2-9, *II Thessalonians 2:1-11, I Timothy 4:1-2, II Timothy 4:3-4 and Hebrews 6: 4-9); *Apostle Peter* (II Peter 2:20-22) and *Apostle Jude* (Jude 1:5). **Spirit of Slumber** (Isaiah 29:10 and Roman 11:8)

The Great Apostasy in Christianity is the fallen away from the Faith during the (End Times) before Jesus Christ Second Advent. God warned against this in the Old Testament, Jesus teaches His Disciples and Apostle Paul wrote to the Thessalonians on the emphasis of Jesus's teaching about this subject. I start in the Old Testament because Jesus tells His Disciples some very important information while at the same time reminding them He has told them things before: Mark 13:20-23 (KJV) says "And except that the Lord had shortened those days, no flesh should be saved: but for the elect's sake, whom he hath chosen, he hath shortened the days. ²¹ And then if any man shall say to you, Lo, here is Christ; or, lo, he is there; believe him not: ²² For false Christs and false prophets shall rise, and shall shew signs and wonders, to seduce, if it were possible, even the elect. ²³ But take ye heed: behold, I have foretold you all things." In addition, when Jesus's Disciples would have a question (s), depending on the subject He would answer first by saying "have you not read?" That's an important question for us also, because God said in Ecclesiastes 1:9 (KJV) says "The thing that hath been, it is that which shall be; and that which is done is that which shall be done: and there is no new thing under the sun." For those of you who believe in the "Rapture," I would say what is the "Armour of God" for and did Jesus mentioned or hint that there would be a "Flying Away?" Oh, God said something against it in: Ezekiel 13: 17-23 (KJV) says "Likewise, thou son of man, set thy face against the daughters of thy people, which prophesy out of their own heart; and prophesy thou against them, [18] And say, Thus saith the Lord GOD; Woe to the women that sew pillows to all armholes and make kerchiefs upon the head of every stature to hunt souls! Will ye hunt the souls of my people, and will ye save the souls alive that come unto you? [19] And will ye pollute me among my people for handfuls of barley and for pieces of bread, to slay the souls that should not die, and to save the souls alive that should not live, by your lying to my people that hear your lies? [20] Wherefore thus saith the Lord GOD; Behold, I am against your pillows, wherewith ye there hunt the souls to make them fly, and I will tear them from your arms, and will let the souls go, even the souls that ye hunt to make them fly. [21] Your kerchiefs also will I tear, and deliver my people out of your hand, and they shall be no more in your hand to be hunted; and ye shall know that I am the LORD. [22] Because with lies ye have made the heart of the righteous sad, whom I have not made sad; and strengthened the hands of the wicked, that he should not return from his wicked way, by promising him life: [23] Therefore ye shall see no more vanity, nor divine divinations: for I will deliver my people out of your hand: and ye shall know that I am the LORD."

Note

The funning thing about what God had said about "Daughter," the actual daughter He spoke of was (Margaret MacDonald) whom had a bad dream and the Rapture Theory was birth by two preachers who overheard her tell someone about her dream. The preachers put it out there as though they had a revelation, but unaware of what God had already told Ezekiel the Prophet He was against it. The sad thing is that the Rapture Theory is still taught and much alive.

II Chronicles 1-15 (KJV) says: "And the Spirit of God came upon Azariah the son of Oded: [2] And he went out to meet Asa, and said unto him, Hear ye me, Asa, and all Judah and Benjamin; The LORD is with you, while ye be with him; and if ye seek him, he will be found of you; but if ye forsake him, he will forsake you. ³ Now for a long season Israel hath been without the true God, and without a teaching priest, and without law. ⁴ But when they in their trouble did turn unto the LORD God of Israel, and sought him, he was found of them. ⁵ And in those times there was no peace to him that went out, nor to him that came in, but great vexations were upon all the inhabitants of the countries. ⁶ And nation was destroyed of nation, and city of city: for God did vex them with all adversity. ⁷ Be ye strong therefore, and let not your hands be weak: for your work shall be rewarded. ⁸ And when Asa heard these words, and the prophecy of Oded the prophet, he took courage, and put away the abominable idols out of all the land of Judah and Benjamin, and out of the cities which he had taken from mount Ephraim, and renewed the altar of the LORD, that was before the porch of the LORD. ⁹ And he gathered all Judah and Benjamin, and the strangers with them out of Ephraim and Manasseh, and out of Simeon: for they fell to him out of Israel in abundance, when they saw that the LORD his God was with him. ¹⁰ So they gathered themselves together at Jerusalem in the third month, in the fifteenth year of the reign of Asa. ¹¹ And they offered unto the LORD the same time, of the spoil which they had brought, seven hundred oxen and seven thousand sheep. ¹² And they entered into a covenant to seek the LORD God of their fathers with all their heart and with all their soul; ¹³ That whosoever would not seek the LORD God of Israel should be put to death, whether small or great, whether man or woman. ¹⁴ And they sware unto the LORD with a loud voice, and with shouting, and with trumpets, and with cornets. ¹⁵ And all Judah rejoiced at the oath: for they had sworn with all their heart, and sought him with their whole desire; and he was found of them: and the LORD gave them rest round about."

Deuteronomy 13: 1-18 (KJV) says "If there arise among you a prophet, or a dreamer of dreams, and giveth thee a sign or a wonder, ² And the sign or the wonder come to pass, whereof he spake unto thee, saying, Let us go after other gods, which thou hast not known, and let us serve them; ³ Thou shalt not hearken unto the words of that prophet, or that dreamer of dreams: for the LORD your God proveth you, to know whether ye love the LORD your God with all your heart and with all your soul. ⁴ Ye shall walk after the LORD your God, and fear him, and keep his commandments, and obey his voice, and ye shall serve him, and cleave unto him. ⁵ And that prophet, or that dreamer of dreams, shall be put to death; because he hath spoken to turn you away from the LORD your God, which brought you out of the land of Egypt, and redeemed you out of the house of bondage, to thrust thee out of the way which the LORD thy God commanded thee to walk in. So shalt thou put the evil away from the midst of thee. ⁶ If thy brother, the son of thy mother, or thy son, or thy daughter, or the wife of thy bosom, or thy friend, which is as thine own soul, entice thee secretly, saying, Let us go and serve other gods, which thou hast not known, thou, nor thy fathers; ⁷ Namely, of the gods of the people which are round about you, nigh unto thee, or far off from thee, from the one end of the earth even unto the other end of the earth; ⁸ Thou shalt not consent unto him, nor hearken unto him; neither shall thine eye pity him, neither shalt thou spare, neither shalt thou conceal him: ⁹ But thou shalt surely kill him; thine hand shall be first upon him to put him to death, and afterwards the hand of all the people. ¹⁰ And thou shalt stone him with stones, that he die; because he hath sought to thrust thee away from the LORD thy God, which brought thee out of the land of Egypt, from the house of bondage. ¹¹ And all Israel shall hear, and fear, and shall do no more any such wickedness as this is among you. ¹² If thou shalt hear say in one of thy cities, which the LORD thy God hath given thee to dwell there, saying, ¹³ Certain men, the children of Belial, are gone out from among you, and have withdrawn the inhabitants of their city, saying, Let us go and serve other gods, which ye have not known; ¹⁴ Then shalt thou inquire, and make search, and ask diligently; and, behold, if it be truth, and the thing certain, that such abomination is wrought among you; ¹⁵ Thou shalt surely smite the inhabitants of that city with the edge of the sword, destroying it utterly, and all that is therein, and the cattle thereof, with the edge of the sword. ¹⁶ And thou shalt gather all the spoil of it into the midst of the street thereof, and shalt burn with fire the city, and all the spoil thereof every whit, for the LORD thy God: and it shall be an heap forever; it shall not be built again. ¹⁷ And there shall cleave nought of the cursed thing to thine hand: that the LORD may turn from the fierceness of his anger, and show thee mercy, and have compassion upon thee, and multiply thee, as he hath sworn unto thy fathers; ¹⁸ When thou shalt hearken to the voice of the LORD thy God, to keep all his commandments which I command thee this day, to do that which is right in the eyes of the LORD thy God."

Matthew 24: 3-14 (KJV) says "And as he sat upon the mount of Olives, the disciples came unto him privately, saying, Tell us, when shall these things be? and what shall be the sign of thy coming, and of the end of the world? [4] And Jesus answered and said unto them, Take heed that no man deceive you. [5] For many shall come in my name, saying, I am Christ; and shall deceive many. [6] And ye shall hear of wars and rumours of wars: see that ye be not troubled: for all these things must come to pass, but the end is not yet. [7] For nation shall rise against nation, and kingdom against kingdom: and there shall be famines, and pestilences, and earthquakes, in divers' places. [8] All these are the beginning of sorrows. [9] Then shall they deliver you up to be afflicted, and shall kill you: and ye shall be hated of all nations for my name's sake. [10] And then shall many be offended, and shall betray one another, and shall hate one another. [11] And many false prophets shall rise, and shall deceive many. [12] And because iniquity shall abound, the love of many shall wax cold. [13] But he that shall endure unto the end, the same shall be saved. [14] And this gospel of the kingdom shall be preached in all the world for a witness unto all nations; and then shall the end come."

Luke 8: 11-15 (KJV) is the Explanation of the Parable of the (Sower): "Now the parable is this: The seed is the word of God. [12] Those by the wayside are they that hear; then cometh the devil, and taketh away the word out of their hearts, lest they should believe and be saved.[13] They on the rock are they, which, when they hear, receive the word with joy; and these have no root, which for a while believe, and in time of temptation fall away. [14] And that which fell among thorns are they, which, when they have heard, go forth, and are choked with cares and riches and pleasures of this life, and bring no fruit to perfection. [15] But that on the good ground are they, which in an honest and good heart, having heard the word, keep it, and bring forth fruit with patience."

Note: Also in Matthew 13: 18-23 (KJV) and Mark 4: 13-20 (KJV)!

John 6:63-70 (KJV) says "It is the spirit that quickeneth; the flesh profiteth nothing: the words that I speak unto you, they are spirit, and they are life. [64] But there are some of you that believe not. For Jesus knew from the beginning who they were that believed not, and who should betray him. [65] And he said, Therefore said I unto you, that no man can come unto me, except it were given unto him of my Father. [66] From that time many of his disciples went back, and walked no more with him. [67] Then said Jesus unto the twelve, Will ye also go away? [68] Then Simon Peter answered him, Lord, to whom shall we go? thou hast the words of eternal life. [69] And we believe and are sure that thou art that Christ, the Son of the living God. [70] Jesus answered them, Have not I chosen you twelve, and one of you is a devil?"

Galatians 1: 1-9 (KJV) says "Paul, an apostle, (not of men, neither by man, but by Jesus Christ, and God the Father, who raised him from the dead);A) [2] And all the brethren which are with me, unto the churches of Galatia: [3] Grace be to you and peace from God the Father, and from our Lord Jesus Christ, [4] Who gave himself for our sins, that he might deliver us from this present evil world, according to the will of God and our Father: [5] To whom be glory for ever and ever. Amen. [6] I marvel that ye are so soon removed from him that called you into the grace of Christ unto another gospel: [7] Which is not another; but there be some that trouble you, and would pervert the gospel of Christ. [8] But though we, or an angel from heaven, preach any other gospel unto you than that which we have preached unto you, let him be accursed. [9] As we said before, so say I now again, if any man preach any other gospel unto you than that ye have received, let him be accursed."

II Thessalonians 2: 1-11 (KJV) says "Now we beseech you, brethren, by the coming of our Lord Jesus Christ, and by our gathering together unto him, [2] That ye be not soon shaken in mind, or be troubled, neither by spirit, nor by word, nor by letter as from us, as that the day of Christ is at hand. [3] Let no man deceive you by any means: for that day shall not come, except there come a falling away first, and that man of sin be revealed, the son of perdition; [4] Who opposeth and exalteth himself above all that is called God, or that is worshipped; so that he as God sitteth in the temple of God, shewing himself that he is God. [5] Remember ye not, that, when I was yet with you, I told you these things? ⁶ And now ye know what withholdeth that he might be revealed in his time. ⁷ For the mystery of iniquity doth already work: only he who now letteth will let, until he be taken out of the way. ⁸ And then shall that Wicked be revealed, whom the Lord shall consume with the spirit of his mouth, and shall destroy with the brightness of his coming: ⁹ Even him, whose coming is after the working of Satan with all power and signs and lying wonders, ¹⁰ And with all deceivableness of unrighteousness in them that perish; because they received not the love of the truth, that they might be saved. ¹¹ And for this cause God shall send them strong delusion, that they should believe a lie:"

Note

In verse eleven *"Strong Delusion"* was given because of verse ten! Delusion: an idiosyncratic belief or impression that is firmly maintained despite being contradicted by what is generally accepted as reality or rational argument, typically a symptom of mental disorder. Question: Have you ever seen a person or people walking around like they have no clue on what's going on around them? HMM!

I Timothy 4: 1-2 (KJV) says "Now the Spirit speaketh expressly, that in the latter times some shall depart from the faith, giving heed to seducing spirits, and doctrines of devils; ² Speaking lies in hypocrisy; having their conscience seared with a hot iron;"

II Timothy 4: 3-4 (KJV) says "For the time will come when they will not endure sound doctrine; but after their own lusts shall they heap to themselves teachers, having itching ears; ⁴ And they shall turn away their ears from the truth, and shall be turned unto fables."

Hebrew 6: 4-9 (KJV) says "For it is impossible for those who were once enlightened, and have tasted of the heavenly gift, and were made partakers of the Holy Ghost, ⁵ And have tasted the good word of God, and the powers of the world to come, ⁶ If they shall fall away, to renew them again unto repentance; seeing they crucify to themselves the Son of God afresh, and put him to an open shame. ⁷ For the earth which drinketh in the rain that cometh oft upon it, and bringeth forth herbs meet for them by whom it is dressed, receiveth blessing from God: ⁸ But that which beareth thorns and briers is rejected, and is nigh unto cursing; whose end is to be burned. ⁹ But, beloved, we are persuaded better things of you, and things that accompany salvation, though we thus speak."

II Peter 2: 20-22 (KJV) says "For if after they have escaped the pollutions of the world through the knowledge of the Lord and Savior Jesus Christ, they are again entangled therein, and overcome, the latter end is worse with them than the beginning. ²¹ For it had been better for them not to have known the way of righteousness, than, after they have known it, to turn from the holy commandment delivered unto them. ²² But it is happened unto them according to the true proverb, The dog is turned to his own vomit again; and the sow that was washed to her wallowing in the mire."

Jude 1:5 (KJV) says "I will therefore put you in remembrance, though ye once knew this, how that the Lord, having saved the people out of the land of Egypt, afterward destroyed them that believed not."

Spirit of Slumber

When God's Spirit is poured out on a person (people) they will be in a state of inactivity, negligence, quiescence, or calm Sleep. They are asleep to the knowledge of the LORD (YHVH), but very much awake to the way of the world in unrighteousness!

Isaiah 29: 7-10 (KJV) says "And the multitude of all the nations that fight against Ariel, even all that fight against her and her munition, and that distress her, shall be as a dream of a night vision. ⁸ It shall even be as when an hungry man dreameth, and, behold, he eateth; but he awaketh, and his soul is empty: or as when a thirsty man dreameth, and, behold, he drinketh; but he awaketh, and, behold, he is faint, and his soul hath appetite: so shall the multitude of all the nations be, that fight against mount Zion. ⁹ Stay yourselves, and wonder; cry ye out, and cry: they are drunken, but not with wine; they stagger, but not with strong drink. ¹⁰ For the LORD hath poured out upon you the spirit of deep sleep, and hath closed your eyes: the prophets and your rulers, the seers hath he covered."

Roman 11:1-8 (KJV) says "I say then, Hath God cast away his people? God forbid. For I also am an Israelite, of the seed of Abraham, of the tribe of Benjamin. ² God hath not cast away his people which he foreknew. Wot ye not what the scripture saith of Elias? how he maketh intercession to God against Israel saying, ³ Lord, they have killed thy prophets, and digged down thine altars; and I am left alone, and they seek my life. ⁴ But what saith the answer of God unto him? I have reserved to myself seven thousand men, who have not bowed the knee to the image of Baal. ⁵ Even so then at this present time also there is a remnant according to the election of grace. ⁶ And if by grace, then is it no more of works: otherwise grace is no more grace. But if it be of works, then it is no more grace: otherwise work is no more work. ⁷ What then? Israel hath not obtained that which he seeketh for; but the election hath obtained it, and the rest were blinded. ⁸ (According as it is written, God hath given them the spirit of slumber, eyes that they should not see, and ears that they should not hear;) unto this day."

"666" (6th Seal, 6th Trumpet, and 6th Vial) - You need to know God's Plan!

Revelation 6:12-17 (KJV) and, Revelation 7:4-10, 9:13-21, and 16:12-21 (KJV) explains the 144,000 from the tribes of Israel and the Other Nations. Read the entire Chapters!

CHAPTER 5

(FIFTH TRUMPET) - THE LOCUST ARMY {REVELATION 9: 1-12 (KJV)} - WHO ARE THESE LOCUSTS? HMM - GOD'S ARMY!

There're men, coming to torment all those that don't have the "Seal of God" in their forehead. Prophesy had been given in the Old Testament by God through His Prophet Joel in Joel 2:25 (KJV) "And I will restore to you the years that the locust hath eaten, the cankerworm, and the caterpillar, and the palmerworm, My great army which I sent among you." Revelation 9:1-12 (KJV) says "And the fifth angel sounded, and I saw a star fall from heaven unto the earth: and to him was given the key of the bottomless pit. ² And he opened the bottomless pit; and there arose a smoke out of the pit, as the smoke of a great furnace; and the sun and the air were darkened by reason of the smoke of the pit. ³ And there came out of the smoke locusts upon the earth: and unto them was given power, as the scorpions of the earth have power. ⁴ And it was commanded them that they should not hurt the grass of the earth, neither any green thing, neither any tree; but only those men which have not the seal of God in their foreheads. ⁵ And to them it was given that they should not kill them, but that they should be tormented five months: and their torment was as the torment of a scorpion, when he striketh a man. ⁶ And in those days shall men seek death, and shall not find it; and shall desire to die, and death shall flee from them. ⁷ And the shapes of the locusts were like unto horses prepared unto battle; and on their heads were as it were crowns like gold, and their faces were as the faces of men. [8] And they had hair as the hair of women, and their teeth were as the teeth of lions. [9] And they had breastplates, as it were breastplates of iron; and the sound of their wings was as the sound of chariots of many horses running to battle. [10] And they had tails like unto scorpions, and there were stings in their tails: and their power was to hurt men five months. [11] And they had a king over them, which is the angel of the bottomless pit, whose name in the Hebrew tongue is Abaddon, but in the Greek tongue hath his name Apollyon. [12] One woe is past; and, behold, there come two woes more hereafter."

NOTE: God uses Satan's seed the (Kenites–Sons of Cain) as the negative part of God's plan to bring His people Israel back to Him; and the Four Stages of the Locust Army is intellectual to God's End time Plan for Salvation. In Joel 1:4 (KJV) Joel describes the four stages in a locust's life. Keep in mind these locusts are Kenites, the seed of Satan. In a sense this verse warns of the one world government system, described in Revelation that shall take over the monetary system and control of the world, until the tree is debarked with nothing left. Joel tells us these words, but the word come from the Father. In this chapter, God says a nation is come up upon His land. Joel 1:6 (KJV) says "Tells us that the locust has made it bare." If you have studied Revelation 9, this speaks unmistakably of the Kenites nation and their father, Satan. It is they who own our homes, our cars and our pastures through usury and taxation. They owned our governments through bribery and manipulation. Joel 2:1 (KJV) says "Blow ye the trumpet in Zion, and sound an alarm in my holy mountain: let all the inhabitants of the land tremble: for the day of the LORD cometh, for it is nigh at hand;"

Who are the locusts? Joel 2:11 (KJV) says "And the LORD shall utter his voice before his army: for his camp is very great: for he is strong that executeth his word: for the day of the LORD is great and very terrible; and who can abide it?" Joel 2:25 (KJV) says "And I will restore to you the years that the locust hath eaten, the cankerworm, and the caterpiller, and the palmerworm, My great army which I sent among you?"

You can read more about the "Locust Army" and their description in Revelation 9:7-10 (KJV), and through their deception they can and may lead you to sacrifice your opportunity for eternal life!

These are the four stages of the "Locust", in the Hebrew it really says:

(1) Gnawer's remnant; (2) Swarmer eats & Swarmer's remnant; (3) Devourer eats & Devourers remnant and (4) Consumer eats

<u>Palmerworm is the Gnawer</u> - (Gazam in Hebrew) <u>Gazam</u>- to rob, take violently, spoil, to devour, to cut down. *Gnawer* as the first stage is the Conspiracy against God's children, deception of their lies, false teaching, ripping people off, new laws to enforce the people to do things against their religious beliefs, they fine and tax businesses right out of business.

Gazam- The government is robbing us and taking us for granted and our spoils which we work hard for. They set laws that we don't vote for or on, they divide between what is right and wrong and make people to believe that it is right while they do wrong and slowly (in some cases quickly) snatching all our rights, so eventually we will have no say in what happens even if we do have something to say. The brainwashing is in full motion and many believe it is the right way. **Can you not see how much we are going astray from God?**

<u>Locust is the Swarmer</u> - (Arbeh in Hebrew) – Second stage the Swarmers - Locust means Arabia's, the imago stage, their sounds were peace, peace but what do they do? **Arbeh**- a rapid increase **(Arab):** In addition: <u>Tsalal</u>- rattle together, ears reddening with shame, teeth chattering, to tumble down or sink, begin to darken or illusion. In today's' world we see a rapid increase in violence, riots and cries for peace, peace around the world. A lot of people are desensitized to the Word of God and believe in political correctness. **Perversion** is okay and not punished (men marrying men and women marrying women) to where all the perverts are coming out of the woodwork. There are so many murderers and rapists, but if we do according to the Bible—Execute them when found guilty without any reason of doubt – God said this would cease to be. In addition, our

government, education, media etc., has put forth an illusion as not to offend or they put forth their agenda for gain. Our economy and our thoughts our sinking and beginning to be darkened.

Cankerworm is the Devourer – **(Yelek in Hebrew)** is to lick up like a dog; Yalal- to utter inconsiderately, devour, to howl or howling; Yalak- to carry or bear! Yelek- the government takes as much as they can just like a dog licking up something that spills on the floor. They are so inconsiderate how much it will cost us, because ultimately, we as tax payers will pay for it (Just as President Trump wants American tax payers to pay for his wall, but he lied and said Mexico will pay for it). We are seeing this third stage of the locusts – Cankerworm (s) as the Devourer at their best now. They are working overtime to take over the USA and bring in One world Order. Some powerful people play right into One Worldism or New World Order under one god, their god; but God said it would happen so don't be so surprised. Finally, we bear the burden of all their bad decisions.

Hmm! The Cankerworm or better said "The Moth" and the Hebrew the word for cankerworm is *yelek* mean young **locust** or **locust larvae** but what the Moth signifies throughout the Word of God will amaze you. Example: In Hosea 5:12 (KJV) God said, "Therefore will I be unto Ephraim as a moth, and to the house of Judah as rottenness." Ephraim is symbolical of the United States and Judah is Jerusalem; therefore, read chapter five in its entirety. Jesus said in Matthew 6:19-21 (KJV) says "Lay not up for yourselves treasures upon earth, where moth and rust doth corrupt, and where thieves break through and steal: [20] But lay up for yourselves treasures in heaven, where neither moth nor rust doth corrupt, and where thieves do not break through nor steal: [21] For where your treasure is, there will your heart be also." In James chapter five this Moth's role is revealed, it is symbolic of our monetary system and the corruption of the men that run it. James 5: 1-6 (KJV) Jesus' half-brother James says "Go to now, ye rich men, weep and howl for your miseries that shall come upon you. [2] Your riches are corrupted, and your garments are motheaten. [3] Your gold and silver is cankered; and the rust of them shall be a witness against you, and shall eat your flesh as it were fire. Ye have heaped treasure together for the last days. [4] Behold, the hire of the labourers who have reaped down your fields, which is of you kept back by fraud, crieth: and the cries of them which have reaped are entered into the ears of the Lord of sabaoth. [5] Ye have lived in pleasure on the earth, and been wanton; ye have nourished your hearts, as in a day of slaughter. [6] Ye have condemned and killed the just; and he doth not resist you."

What does a Moth eat? A Moth eats linen, wool and mainly cotton and they like dirty fabrics that have sweat in them, the Moth larvae needs this moisture from the sweat because they do not drink water. Question: What is going on right now around the World with our monetary system? It is being eaten away like a Moth that eats away at the fabric.

Note

Our United States currency paper is composed of 75% cotton and 25% linen.

The analogy is that this Moth is and will destroying our money, slowly but surely the banking system will crash to no return as the Word of God declares, read James chapter five in its entirety and absorb it. We are heading for some tough times, but God will always take care of those who love Him and study His Word, so we have nothing to worry about. Interesting times we live in, stay focused and Watch!

Caterpillar is the Consumer - (Hasil in Hebrew) Hasil- to eat off, consume, consumer, deficient, fail, lacking, destitute, poverty; Halak- toll on goods at a road, taxation. This is the Fourth Stage Caterpillar as the Consumers - the fallen angels spoken of in Jude! This has not happened again yet but will when the 5th trump sounds/becomes a reality - the five months that Jesus shorten because the Flesh cannot handle Satan and his supernatural creatures. Many will appeal by the sound of their wings. False wings, They claim to be pastors, a man of God, but they are false prophets Matthew 24 (KJV), Luke 21 (KJV), & Mark 13 (KJV), and Revelation 9:5-6 (KJV) says "And to them it was given that they should not kill them, but that they should be tormented five months: and their torment was as the torment of a scorpion, when he striketh a man. [6] And in those days shall men seek death and shall not find it; and shall desire to die, and death shall flee from them." Another must read is The parables of the Sower in Matthew 13 (KJV), when you sowed seed (teach God's Word), "some seeds fell by the wayside because of false teaching." In addition, Hasil-The government consumes all the wealth and profits and tells us as consumers to spend more that we don't have and further the problem of debt, which makes us fail as a nation. We lack the things we used to have: a roof over our heads, employment, health care, etc. It makes some people destitute for relief and finally poverty stricken, literally and spiritually. Socialism begins to creep in and our need for Government aid increases to the point of almost collapsing our Democracy. Gazar- divide, decree, snatch.

Notes

The Lord uses things of nature that most people are familiar with, so His word can understood. God likened the deception to a *flight of locusts*, whereby you can identify with the things you can see. Although you can see locusts, the *flight of locusts* is pertaining to a length of time. That length of time is five months May through September, and any of length of time the people would be harvest out of season. Jesus mentioned shorting the time for the Elect's sake and you can find that shorten time in Revelation 9: 5a (KJV) that says "And to them it was given that they should not kill them, but that they should be tormented five months."

Locusts come from underground which means, they (their rulers) go behind closed doors, these men say one thing and do something else. If you have not read God's word, you won't know what's going on when Satan is cast out of heaven! Revelation 12 (KJV), and Revelation 9 (KJV) say these Locusts come in groups (from their rapid increase) and try to destroy everything in their path. These Locusts are Kenites (sons of Cain) who have mixed with all races will have a gentle appearance shown by the reference to having (hair of women); but their flattery will deceive many with their false gentleness, and their teachings and actions will have the same effect as a lion when it attacks.

God said to Jeremiah in Jeremiah 4:22 (KJV) "For my people is foolish, they have not known me; they are sottish children, and they have none understanding they are wise to do evil, but to do good they have no knowledge." Sottish means To be silly or to be Stupid! These locusts are men, It is very clear in Revelation 9 (KJV) that those locusts are examples, and we are talking about men, not insects.

6th Seal–*Affix/Seal these Words in our mind to be Aware what is happening and not to be Deceived!*

Revelation 6:12-17 (KJV) says "And I beheld when he had opened the sixth seal, and, lo, there was a great earthquake; and the sun became black as sackcloth of hair, and the moon became as blood; [13] And the stars of heaven fell unto the earth, even as a fig tree casteth her untimely figs, when she is shaken of a mighty wind. [14] And the heaven departed as a scroll when it is rolled together; and every mountain and island were moved out of their places. [15] And the kings of the earth, and the great men, and the rich men, and the chief captains, and the mighty men, and every bondman, and every free man, hid themselves in the dens and in the rocks of the mountains; [16] And said to the mountains and rocks, Fall on us, and hide us from the face of him that sitteth on the throne, and from the wrath of the Lamb: [17] For the great day of his wrath is come; and who shall be able to stand?"

144,000 Israelites Sealed: {12 Tribes x 12,000} ((+) All other Nations/ People

Revelation 7:4-10 (KJV) says "And I heard the number of them which were sealed: and there were sealed an hundred and forty and four thousand of all the tribes of the children of Israel. [5] Of the tribe of Juda were sealed twelve thousand. Of the tribe of Reuben were sealed twelve thousand. Of the tribe of Gad were sealed twelve thousand. [6] Of the tribe of Aser were sealed twelve thousand. Of the tribe of Nephthalim were sealed twelve thousand. Of the tribe of Manasses were sealed twelve thousand. [7] Of the tribe of Simeon were sealed twelve thousand. Of the tribe of Levi were sealed twelve thousand. Of the tribe of Issachar were sealed twelve thousand. [8] Of the tribe of Zabulon were sealed twelve thousand. Of the tribe of Joseph were sealed twelve thousand. Of the tribe of Benjamin were sealed twelve thousand. [9] After this I beheld, and, lo, a great multitude, which no man could number, of all nations, and kindreds, and people, and tongues, stood before the throne, and before the Lamb, clothed with white robes, and palms in their hands; [10] And cried with a loud voice, saying, Salvation to our God which sitteth upon the throne, and unto the Lamb."

6th Trumpet- This trumpet is not literally a trump that make a sound, it's an Execution Alarm/Warning for what is about to happen/take place!

Revelation 9:13-21 (KJV) says "And the sixth angel sounded, and I heard a voice from the four horns of the golden altar which is before God, [14] Saying to the sixth angel which had the trumpet, Loose the four angels which are bound in the great river Euphrates. [15] And the four angels were loosed, which were prepared for an hour, and a day, and a month, and a year, for to slay the third part of men. [16] And the number of the army of the horsemen were two hundred thousand thousand: and I heard the number of them. [17] And thus I saw the horses in the vision, and them that sat on them, having breastplates of fire, and of jacinth, and brimstone: and the heads of the horses were as the heads of lions; and out of their mouths issued fire and smoke and brimstone. [18] By these three was the third part of men killed, by the fire, and by the smoke, and by the brimstone, which issued out of their mouths.

[19] For their power is in their mouth, and in their tails: for their tails were like unto serpents, and had heads, and with them they do hurt. [20] And the rest of the men which were not killed by these plagues yet repented not of the works of their hands, that they should not worship devils, and idols of gold, and silver, and brass, and stone, and of wood: which neither can see, nor hear, nor walk: [21] Neither repented they of their murders, nor of their sorceries, nor of their fornication, nor of their thefts."

6th Vial – In this case it's a wide mouth glass and what's in it will be emptied fast & quickly!

Revelation 16:12-21 (KJV) says "And the sixth angel poured out his vial upon the great river Euphrates; and the water thereof was dried up, that the way of the kings of the east might be prepared. [13] And I saw three unclean spirits like frogs come out of the mouth of the dragon, and out of the mouth of the beast, and out of the mouth of the false prophet. [14] For they are the spirits of devils, working miracles, which go forth unto the kings of the earth and of the whole world, to gather them to the battle of that great day of God Almighty. [15] Behold, I come as a thief. Blessed is he that watcheth, and keepeth his garments, lest he walk naked, and they see his shame. [16] And he gathered them together into a place called in the Hebrew tongue Armageddon. [17] And the seventh angel poured out his vial into the air; and there came a great voice out of the temple of heaven, from the throne, saying, It is done. [18] And there were voices, and thunders, and lightnings; and there was a great earthquake, such as was not since men were upon the earth, so mighty an earthquake, and so great. [19] And the great city was divided into three parts, and the cities of the nations fell: and great Babylon came in remembrance before God, to give unto her the cup of the wine of the fierceness of his wrath. [20] And every island fled away, and the mountains were not found. [21] And there fell upon men a great hail out of heaven, every stone about the weight of a talent: and men blasphemed God because of the plague of the hail; for the plague thereof was exceeding great."

CHAPTER 6

ARMAGEDDON AND HAYMENGOG

Revelation 16:16 (KJV), and Ezekiel 38-39 (KJV)

Note

In 1867 the United States brought Alaska from Russia for 7.2 million dollars; not knowing it was in God's plan for that to happen and its final purpose is to be the burial ground for Esau and Cain's descendants (those who don't believe in Jesus Christ).

Armageddon

This frightening apocalyptic word *"Armageddon"* refers to earth's final battle which is generally referred to as the *"Battle of Armageddon."* But who are the contestants of this great battle of Armageddon? A common reply would be *"Russia, Syria,* and or *Iran* against *Israel."* As the Middle East simmers toward a boiling point, and as U.S., British, and Israeli intelligence monitor closely Iran's quest for a nuclear bomb which might even be used against America. Millions of Christians, Jews, Muslims, and even secularists are pondering, "Is the Battle of Armageddon at hand?" I believe so. Valley of Megiddo and where some believe the battle of Armageddon will be?

The word *"Armageddon"* appears only once in the entire Bible and is found in Revelation 16:16 (KJV). If you open God's Word and read this passage yourself along with the verses at once before and after it, you will be amazed at what you will find and not find in regard to the *"Battle of Armageddon."* Look for yourself:

Interestingly, no place on earth bears the name Armageddon, and the above passage is the only mention of it in scripture. The Greek is most commonly thought to be a transliteration of the Hebrew word har megiddo, literally, *"Mountain of Megiddo."*

Here is what Strong's has to say about the word: Greek# (717) Armageddōn ar-mag-ed-dohn' of Hebrew origin [Hebrew# (2022)] and [Hebrew# (4023)]; Armageddon (or Har-Megiddon), a symbolical name: – Armageddon. Strong's proposes that the Greek word Armageddon originates from the two following Hebrew words: Hebrew# (2022) har A shortened form of Hebrew# (2042); a mountain or range of hills (sometimes used figuratively): – hill (country), mount (-ain), X promotion. Hebrew# (4023) megiddôn megiddô meg-id-done', meg-id-do' From Hebrew# (1413); rendezvous; Megiddon or Megiddo, a place in Palestine: – Megiddo, Megiddon.

The *"Mount of Megiddo"* is in the plain of Esdraelon or Jezreel, a valley fourteen by twenty miles in size located to the southwest of Nazareth. Mount of Megiddo is not actually a mountain, but a tell (a hill created by many generations of people living and rebuilding on the same spot) on which ancient forts were built to guard the Via Maris, an ancient trade route linking Egypt with the northern empire of Syria, Anatolia and Mesopotamia. Megiddo was the location of various ancient battles, including one in the 15th century BC and one in 609 BC. Modern Megiddo is a town approximately 40 kilometers (25 mi) west-southwest of the southern tip of the Sea of Galilee in the Kishon River area in Israel: Here, it is thought by many, that the great final battle of Armageddon will be fought at the end of time.

Matthew 24:29-31 (KJV) says "Immediately after the Tribulation of those days shall the sun be darkened, and the moon shall not give her light, and the stars shall fall from heaven, and the powers of the heavens shall be shaken: 30 And then shall appear the sign of the Son of Man in heaven: and then shall all the tribes of the earth mourn, and they shall see the Son of man coming in the clouds of heaven with power and great glory. [31] And he shall send his angels with a great sound of a trumpet, and they shall gather together his elect from the four winds, from one end of heaven to the other."

Revelation 16:12-21 (KJV) says "And the sixth angel poured out his vial upon the great river Euphrates; and the water thereof was dried up, that the way of the kings of the east might be prepared. [13] And I saw three unclean spirits like frogs come out of the mouth of the dragon, and out of the mouth of the beast, and out of the mouth of the false prophet. [14] For they are the spirits of devils, working miracles, which go forth unto the kings of the earth and of the whole world, to gather them to the battle of that great day of God Almighty. [15]Behold, I come as a thief. Blessed is he that watcheth, and keepeth his garments, lest he walk naked, and they see his shame. [16] And he gathered them together into a place called in the Hebrew tongue Armageddon. [17]And the seventh angel poured out his vial into the air; and there came a great voice out of the temple of heaven, from the throne, saying, It is done. [18] And there were voices, and thunders, and lightnings; and there was a great earthquake, such as was not since men were upon the earth, so mighty an earthquake, and so great. [19] And the great city was divided into three parts, and the cities of the nations fell: and great Babylon came in remembrance before God, to give unto her the cup of the wine of the fierceness of his wrath. [20] And every island fled away, and the mountains were not found. [21]And there fell upon men a great hail out of heaven, every stone about the weight of a talent: and men blasphemed God because of the plague of the hail; for the plague thereof was exceeding great."

According to the *"Book of Revelation"* in the New Testament of the Bible, **Armageddon** (/ˌɑːrməˈɡɛdən/, from Ancient Greek: Ἁρμαγεδών *Harmagedōn*, Late Latin: *Armagedon*, from Hebrew: הר מגידו Har Megiddo) is the prophesied location of a gathering of armies for a battle during the end times, variously interpreted as either a literal or a symbolic location. The term is also used in a generic sense to refer to any end of the world scenario.

Heymengog (Hamon-gog)

Multitude of Gog, the name of the valley in which the slaughtered forces of Gog are to be buried in Ezekiel 39:11&15 (KJV), "the valley of the passengers on the east of the sea." Ezekiel 39:11-15 (KJV) says "And it shall come to pass in that day, that I will give unto Gog a place there of graves in Israel, the valley of the passengers on the east of the sea: and it shall stop the noses of the passengers: and there shall they bury Gog and all his multitude: and they shall call it The valley of Hamongog. 12 And seven months shall the house of Israel be burying of them, that they may cleanse the land. 13 Yea, all the people of the land shall bury them; and it shall be to them a renown the day that I shall be glorified, saith the Lord GOD. 14 And they shall sever out men of continual employment, passing through the land to bury with the passengers those that remain upon the face of the earth, to cleanse it: after the end of seven months shall they search. 15 And the passengers that pass through the land, when any seeth a man's bone, then shall he set up a sign by it, till the buriers have buried it in the valley of Hamongog."

CHAPTER 7

"777" (7ᵀᴴ SEAL, {TWO WITNESSES} THEN 7ᵀᴴ TRUMPET, AND 7ᵀᴴ VIAL)

Revelation 8:1-6; 11and 16:17(KJV)

Revelation 8:1-6 (KJV); (**7ᵗʰ Seal**) says "And when he had opened the seventh seal, there was silence in heaven about the space of half an hour. ² And I saw the seven angels which stood before God; and to them were given seven trumpets. ³ And another angel came and stood at the altar, having a golden censer; and there was given unto him much incense, that he should offer it with the prayers of all saints upon the golden altar which was before the throne. ⁴ And the smoke of the incense, which came with the prayers of the saints, ascended up before God out of the angel's hand. ⁵ And the angel took the censer, and filled it with fire of the altar, and cast it into the earth: and there were voices, and thunderings, and lightnings, and an earthquake. ⁶ And the seven angels which had the seven trumpets prepared themselves to sound."

Revelation 11: 2-9; 12-17 (KJV), and 19 (KJV){Two Witnesses} then (**7ᵗʰ Trumpet**) "But the court which is without the temple leave out, and measure it not; for it is given unto the Gentiles: and the holy city shall they tread under foot forty and two months.{**Note:** This was changed to Five Months} ³ And I will give power unto my two witnesses, and they shall prophesy a thousand two hundred and threescore days, clothed in sackcloth. ⁴ These are the two olive trees, and the two candlesticks standing before the God of the earth. ⁵ And if any man will hurt them, fire proceedeth out of

118

their mouth, and devoureth their enemies: and if any man will hurt them, he must in this manner be killed. ⁶These have power to shut heaven, that it rain not in the days of their prophecy: and have power over waters to turn them to blood, and to smite the earth with all plagues, as often as they will. ⁷And when they shall have finished their testimony, the beast that ascendeth out of the bottomless pit shall make war against them, and shall overcome them, and kill them. ⁸And their dead bodies shall lie in the street of the great city, which spiritually is called Sodom and Egypt, where also our Lord was crucified. ⁹And they of the people and kindreds and tongues and nations shall see their dead bodies three days and an half, and shall not suffer their dead bodies to be put in graves."

¹²"And they heard a great voice from heaven saying unto them, Come up hither. And they ascended up to heaven in a cloud; and their enemies beheld them. ¹³And the same hour was there a great earthquake, and the tenth part of the city fell, and in the earthquake were slain of men seven thousand: and the remnant were affrighted, and gave glory to the God of heaven. ¹⁴The second woe is past; and, behold, the third woe cometh quickly. ¹⁵And the seventh angel sounded (7ᵗʰ Trumpet); and there were great voices in heaven, saying, The kingdoms of this world are become the kingdoms of our Lord, and of his Christ; and he shall reign for ever and ever. ¹⁶And the four and twenty elders, which sat before God on their seats, fell upon their faces, and worshipped God, ¹⁷Saying, We give thee thanks, O LORD God Almighty, which art, and wast, and art to come; because thou hast taken to thee thy great power, and hast reigned."

¹⁹"And the temple of God was opened in heaven, and there was seen in his temple the ark of his testament: and there were lightnings, and voices, and thunderings, and an earthquake, and great hail."

This is when Jesus Christ and His angles (teachers) will arrive on earth and the beginning of the Millennium (One Thousand Years/The Lord's Day) right here on earth. Everything that has breath will be in their spiritual body and the people who did not make the first resurrection (their soul is still mortal) and was on the wrong side of Paradise will be taught the TRUTH.

CHAPTER 8

MILLENNIUM–ONE THOUSAND YEARS (THE LORD'S DAY)

Ezekiel 40-48 (KJV), and Revelation 20 (KJV)

Millennium

There is more in the Old Testament than the New Testament about the Millennium, therefore I suggest that when time permits read all of Ezekiel 40-48 (KJV) because I'm only going to highlight some scriptures within each chapter.

Ezekiel 40: 2-5 (KJV) says "In the visions of God brought he me into the land of Israel, and set me upon a very high mountain, by which was as the frame of a city on the south. ³ And he brought me thither, and, behold, there was a man, whose appearance was like the appearance of brass, with a line of flax in his hand, and a measuring reed; and he stood in the gate. ⁴ And the man said unto me, Son of man, behold with thine eyes, and hear with thine ears, and set thine heart upon all that I shall shew thee; for to the intent that I might shew them unto thee art thou brought hither: declare all that thou seest to the house of Israel."

God begins to show *Ezekiel* that which will be the New Jerusalem in the Eternity; and gave him all the measurements thereof!

Ezekiel 41: 1; 4 and 20-26 (KJV) says "Afterward he brought me to the temple, and measured the posts, six cubits broad on the one side, and six cubits broad on the other side, which was the breadth of the tabernacle. ⁴ So he measured the length thereof, twenty cubits; and the breadth, twenty cubits, before the temple: and he said unto me, This is the most holy place."

²⁰ "From the ground unto above the door were cherubims and palm trees made, and on the wall of the temple. ²¹ The posts of the temple were squared, and the face of the sanctuary; the appearance of the one as the appearance of the other. ²² The altar of wood was three cubits high, and the length thereof two cubits; and the corners thereof, and the length thereof, and the walls thereof, were of wood: and he said unto me, This is the table that is before the Lord. ²³ And the temple and the sanctuary had two doors. ²⁴ And the doors had two leaves apiece, two turning leaves; two leaves for the one door, and two leaves for the other door. ²⁵ And there were made on them, on the doors of the temple, cherubims and palm trees, like as were made upon the walls; and there were thick planks upon the face of the porch without. ²⁶ And there were narrow windows and palm trees on the one side and on the other side, on the sides of the porch, and upon the side chambers of the house, and thick planks."

God continues to show Ezekiel the New Jerusalem in the Eternity; but in this chapter God gives more emphasis on the measurements of the Temple.

Ezekiel 42: 1, 8-9 and 13-14 (KJV) says "Then he brought me forth into the utter court, the way toward the north: and he brought me into the chamber that was over against the separate place, and which was before the building toward the north. ⁸ For the length of the chambers that were in the utter court was fifty cubits: and, lo, before the temple were an hundred cubits. ⁹ And from under these chambers was the entry on the east side, as one goeth into them from the utter court."

¹³ "Then said he unto me, The north chambers and the south chambers, which are before the separate place, they be holy chambers, where the priests that approach unto the Lord shall eat the most holy things: there

shall they lay the most holy things, and the meat offering, and the sin offering, and the trespass offering; for the place is holy. ¹⁴ When the priests enter therein, then shall they not go out of the holy place into the utter court, but there they shall lay their garments wherein they minister; for they are holy; and shall put on other garments, and shall approach to those things which are for the people."

God continues to show Ezekiel the New Jerusalem in the Eternity and brought him to the utter court and into a chamber in a separate place. In the inner house God shows Ezekiel the upper chambers, other chambers with all the measurements thereof. In addition, God show Ezekiel the gates that would be in each direction (east, north, south and west) with their distance from the inner house; and ending it with a wall in all four direction to make a separation between the sanctuary and the profane place!

Ezekiel 43: 1-2; 4-9 and 26-27 (KJV) says "Afterward he brought me to the gate, even the gate that looketh toward the east: ² And, behold, the glory of the God of Israel came from the way of the east: and his voice was like a noise of many waters: and the earth shined with his glory."

⁴ "And the glory of the Lord came into the house by the way of the gate whose prospect is toward the east. ⁵ So the spirit took me up, and brought me into the inner court; and, behold, the glory of the Lord filled the house. ⁶ And I heard him speaking unto me out of the house; and the man stood by me. 7 And he said unto me, Son of man, the place of my throne, and the place of the soles of my feet, where I will dwell in the midst of the children of Israel forever, and my holy name, shall the house of Israel no more defile, neither they, nor their kings, by their whoredom, nor by the carcases of their kings in their high places. ⁸ In their setting of their threshold by my thresholds, and their post by my posts, and the wall between me and them, they have even defiled my holy name by their abominations that they have committed: wherefore I have consumed them in mine anger. ⁹ Now let them put away their whoredom, and the carcases of their kings, far from me, and I will dwell in the midst of them forever."

²⁶ "Seven days shall they purge the altar and purify it; and they shall consecrate themselves. ²⁷ And when these days are expired, it shall be, that upon the eighth day, and so forward, the priests shall make your burnt offerings upon the altar, and your peace offerings; and I will accept you, saith the Lord God."

God continues to show Ezekiel the New Jerusalem in the Eternity; and God tells Ezekiel the measurements of the pattern of the House of Israel. In addition, God has the priests of the Levites in charge of the ordinance of offering for each day of the week. There will be a change for the sprinkling of blood, because all blood and sin ordinances has been done away with because Jesus shed his blood on the cross! Also, the new thing will happen because Jesus is that "Eighth Day" and the New Beginning!

Ezekiel 44: 1-5 (KJV) says "Then he brought me back the way of the gate of the outward sanctuary which looketh toward the east; and it was shut. ² Then said the Lord unto me; This gate shall be shut, it shall not be opened, and no man shall enter in by it; because the Lord, the God of Israel, hath entered in by it, therefore it shall be shut. ³ It is for the prince; the prince, he shall sit in it to eat bread before the Lord; he shall enter by the way of the porch of that gate, and shall go out by the way of the same. ⁴ Then brought he me the way of the north gate before the house: and I looked, and, behold, the glory of the Lord filled the house of the Lord: and I fell upon my face. ⁵ And the Lord said unto me, Son of man, mark well, and behold with thine eyes, and hear with thine ears all that I say unto thee concerning all the ordinances of the house of the Lord, and all the laws thereof; and mark well the entering in of the house, with every going forth of the sanctuary."

God continues to show Ezekiel the New Jerusalem in the Eternity; and tells Ezekiel the measurements between the Gates in each direction (east, north, south & west). In addition, God tells Ezekiel who will be the Keepers of the House, how He it will be kept cleansed and that He will be the "Inheritance of the Levites."

Ezekiel 45: 1-9 (KJV) says "Moreover, when ye shall divide by lot the land for inheritance, ye shall offer an oblation unto the Lord, an holy portion of the land: the length shall be the length of five and twenty thousand reeds, and the breadth shall be ten thousand. This shall be holy in all the borders thereof round about. ² Of this there shall be for the sanctuary five hundred in length, with five hundred in breadth, square round about; and fifty cubits round about for the suburbs thereof. ³ And of this measure shalt thou measure the length of five and twenty thousand, and the breadth of ten thousand: and in it shall be the sanctuary and the most holy place. ⁴ The holy portion of the land shall be for the priests the ministers of the sanctuary, which shall come near to minister unto the Lord: and it shall be a place for their houses, and a holy place for the sanctuary. ⁵ And the five and twenty thousand of length, and the ten thousand of breadth shall also the Levites, the ministers of the house, have for themselves, for a possession for twenty chambers. ⁶ And ye shall appoint the possession of the city five thousand broad, and five and twenty thousand longs, over against the oblation of the holy portion: it shall be for the whole house of Israel. ⁷ And a portion shall be for the prince on the one side and on the other side of the oblation of the holy portion, and of the possession of the city, before the oblation of the holy portion, and before the possession of the city, from the west side westward, and from the east side eastward: and the length shall be over against one of the portions, from the west border unto the east border. ⁸ In the land shall be his possession in Israel: and my princes shall no more oppress my people; and the rest of the land shall they give to the house of Israel according to their tribes. ⁹ Thus saith the Lord God; Let it suffice you, O princes of Israel: remove violence and spoil, and execute judgment and justice, take away your exactions from my people, saith the Lord God."

God continues to show Ezekiel the New Jerusalem in the Eternity; and God tells Ezekiel the measurements of land portion for each Tribe of Israel, and remember the ordinance of offerings for meat, the sprinkling of blood, and sin ordinances has been done away with because Jesus shed his blood on the cross. In addition, God tells Ezekiel

Ezekiel 46: 1-4 and 16-18 (KJV) says "Thus saith the Lord God; The gate of the inner court that looketh toward the east shall be shut the six working days; but on the sabbath it shall be opened, and in the day of the new moon it shall be opened. ² And the prince shall enter by the way of the porch of that gate without, and shall stand by the post of the gate, and the priests shall prepare his burnt offering and his peace offerings, and he shall worship at the threshold of the gate: then he shall go forth; but the gate shall not be shut until the evening. ³ Likewise the people of the land shall worship at the door of this gate before the Lord in the sabbaths and in the new moons. ⁴ And the burnt offering that the prince shall offer unto the Lord in the sabbath day shall be six lambs without blemish, and a ram without blemish.

¹⁶ "Thus saith the Lord God; If the prince give a gift unto any of his sons, the inheritance thereof shall be his sons'; it shall be their possession by inheritance. ¹⁷ But if he give a gift of his inheritance to one of his servants, then it shall be his to the year of liberty; after it shall return to the prince: but his inheritance shall be his sons' for them. ¹⁸ Moreover the prince shall not take of the people's inheritance by oppression, to thrust them out of their possession; but he shall give his sons inheritance out of his own possession: that my people be not scattered every man from his possession."

God tells Ezekiel about the inner and utter court again and what will happen within it in the New Jerusalem in the Eternity. God continues to tell Ezekiel about how the people will enter the gates and how they will be sanctified and by whom; then God goes on to explain about the "Healing and Restoration of the land." Any time God speaks about a lamb without blemish He is referring to Jesus in the future sense!

Ezekiel 47: 1, 8-9; 12-14 and 21-23 (KJV) says "Afterward he brought me again unto the door of the house; and, behold, waters issued out from under the threshold of the house eastward: for the forefront of the house stood toward the east, and the waters came down from under from the right side of the house, at the south side of the altar."

[8] "Then said he unto me, These waters issue out toward the east country, and go down into the desert, and go into the sea: which being brought forth into the sea, the waters shall be healed. [9] And it shall come to pass, that everything that liveth, which moveth, whithersoever the rivers shall come, shall live: and there shall be a very great multitude of fish, because these waters shall come thither: for they shall be healed; and everything shall live whither the river cometh."

[12] "And by the river upon the bank thereof, on this side and on that side, shall grow all trees for meat, whose leaf shall not fade, neither shall the fruit thereof be consumed: it shall bring forth new fruit according to his months, because their waters they issued out of the sanctuary: and the fruit thereof shall be for meat, and the leaf thereof for medicine. [13] Thus saith the Lord God; This shall be the border, whereby ye shall inherit the land according to the twelve tribes of Israel: Joseph shall have two portions. [14] And ye shall inherit it, one as well as another: concerning the which I lifted up mine hand to give it unto your fathers: and this land shall fall unto you for inheritance."

[21] So shall ye divide this land unto you according to the tribes of Israel. [22] And it shall come to pass, that ye shall divide it by lot for an inheritance unto you, and to the strangers that sojourn among you, which shall beget children among you: and they shall be unto you as born in the country among the children of Israel; they shall have inheritance with you among the tribes of Israel. [23] And it shall come to pass, that in what tribe the stranger sojourneth, there shall ye give him his inheritance, saith the Lord God."

God continues to show Ezekiel the New Jerusalem in the Eternity by bring him again to the House, but this time God shows Ezekiel that which shall come from the House: Scriptures 1-12 are about the Healing of the Land by "The Water and The Trees" and Scripture 13-48 is about "The Restoration of the Land and Cities" - the division of it for the Twelve Tribes of Israel and the people thereof.

Ezekiel 48: 1-8, and 11-14 (KJV) says "Now these are the names of the tribes. From the north end to the coast of the way of Hethlon, as one goeth to Hamath, Hazarenan, the border of Damascus northward, to the coast of Hamath; for these are his sides east and west; a portion for Dan. ² And by the border of Dan, from the east side unto the west side, a portion for Asher. ³ And by the border of Asher, from the east side even unto the west side, a portion for Naphtali. ⁴ And by the border of Naphtali, from the east side unto the west side, a portion for Manasseh. ⁵ And by the border of Manasseh, from the east side unto the west side, a portion for Ephraim. ⁶ And by the border of Ephraim, from the east side even unto the west side, a portion for Reuben. ⁷ And by the border of Reuben, from the east side unto the west side, a portion for Judah. ⁸ And by the border of Judah, from the east side unto the west side, shall be the offering which ye shall offer of five and twenty thousand reeds in breadth, and in length as one of the other parts, from the east side unto the west side: and the sanctuary shall be in the midst of it."

¹¹ "It shall be for the priests that are sanctified of the sons of Zadok; which have kept my charge, which went not astray when the children of Israel went astray, as the Levites went astray. ¹² And this oblation of the land that is offered shall be unto them a thing most holy by the border of the Levites. ¹³ And over against the border of the priests the Levites shall have five and twenty thousand in length, and ten thousand in breadth: all the length shall be five and twenty thousand, and the breadth ten thousand. ¹⁴ And they shall not sell of it, neither exchange, nor alienate the first fruits of the land: for it is holy unto the Lord."

God continues to show Ezekiel the New Jerusalem in the Eternity broken down by "Civil"- Introversion by way of The Common Place–of The City sites and their measurements along with its suburbs. Then God goes on to show Ezekiel "The City Exits" through their "Gates" (east, north, south and west) with the measurements between each thereof!

Revelation 20:1-8 (KJV) says "And I saw an angel come down from heaven, having the key of the bottomless pit and a great chain in his hand.

² And he laid hold on the dragon, that old serpent, which is the Devil, and Satan, and bound him a thousand years, ³ And cast him into the bottomless pit, and shut him up, and set a seal upon him, that he should deceive the nations no more, till the thousand years should be fulfilled: and after that he must be loosed a little season. ⁴ And I saw thrones, and they sat upon them, and judgment was given unto them: and I saw the souls of them that were beheaded for the witness of Jesus, and for the word of God, and which had not worshipped the beast, neither his image, neither had received his mark upon their foreheads, or in their hands; and they lived and reigned with Christ a thousand years. ⁵ But the rest of the dead lived not again until the thousand years were finished. This is the first resurrection. ⁶ Blessed and holy is he that hath part in the first resurrection: on such the second death hath no power, but they shall be priests of God and of Christ, and shall reign with him a thousand years. ⁷ And when the thousand years are expired, Satan shall be loosed out of his prison, ⁸ And shall go out to deceive the nations which are in the four quarters of the earth, Gog and Magog, to gather them together to battle: the number of whom is as the sand of the sea.

Now that you have had the chance to read that which I suggested you too, the prophecy given in the Old Testament and the New Testament there's not too much difference. The Old Testament goes into more detail with all the measurements thereof, but no mentioning of Satan; The New Testament has no mentioning of the oblation and offerings, because Jesus covers them all through His "Shed Blood, Death and Resurrection." Therefore all who believe "In" Jesus unto the end shall not Perish but have everlasting Life.

CHAPTER 9

GREAT WHITE THRONE JUDGEMENT!

Revelation 20:11-15(KJV)

Revelation 20: 11-15 (KJV) says "And I saw a great white throne, and him that sat on it, from whose face the earth and the heaven fled away; and there was found no place for them. [12] And I saw the dead, small and great, stand before God; and the books were opened: and another book was opened, which is the book of life: and the dead were judged out of those things which were written in the books, according to their works. [13] And the sea gave up the dead which were in it; and death and hell delivered up the dead which were in them: and they were judged every man according to their works. [14] And death and hell were cast into the lake of fire. This is the second death. [15] And whosoever was not found written in the book of life was cast into the lake of fire."

CHAPTER 10

THE NEW EARTH AND
HEAVEN REJUVENATED

Revelation 21-22 (KJV)

Revelation 21: 1-12 & 21-27 (KJV) says "And I saw a new heaven and a new earth: for the first heaven and the first earth were passed away; and there was no more sea. ² And I John saw the holy city, new Jerusalem, coming down from God out of heaven, prepared as a bride adorned for her husband. ³ And I heard a great voice out of heaven saying, Behold, the tabernacle of God is with men, and he will dwell with them, and they shall be his people, and God himself shall be with them, and be their God. ⁴ And God shall wipe away all tears from their eyes; and there shall be no more death, neither sorrow, nor crying, neither shall there be any more pain: for the former things are passed away. ⁵ And he that sat upon the throne said, Behold, I make all things new. And he said unto me, Write: for these words are true and faithful. ⁶ And he said unto me, It is done. I Am Alpha and Omega, the beginning and the end. I will give unto him that is athirst of the fountain of the water of life freely. ⁷ He that overcometh shall inherit all things; and I will be his God, and he shall be my son. ⁸ But the fearful, and unbelieving, and the abominable, and murderers, and whoremongers, and sorcerers, and idolaters, and all liars, shall have their part in the lake which burneth with fire and brimstone: which is the second death. ⁹ And there came unto me one of the seven angels which had the seven vials full of the seven last plagues, and talked with me, saying, Come hither, I will shew thee the bride, the Lamb's wife. ¹⁰ And he carried me away in the spirit to a great and high mountain, and shewed me that great city, the holy Jerusalem, descending out of heaven from God, [11] Having the glory of God: and her light was like unto a stone most precious, even like a jasper stone, clear as crystal; [12] And had a wall great and high, and had twelve gates, and at the gates twelve angels, and names written thereon, which are the names of the twelve tribes of the children of Israel:"

Note

The earth as it is today will be Rejuvenated back to what it was in the First Earth Age and the waters will return to the firmament and will cover the earth and bring mist to the land to keep it fertile.

[21] "And the twelve gates were twelve pearls: every several gates was of one pearl: and the street of the city was pure gold, as it were transparent glass. (Note: It did not say the whole earth's streets of cities are pure gold as it were transparent glass) [22] And I saw no temple therein: for the Lord God Almighty and the Lamb are the temple of it. [23] And the city had no need of the sun, neither of the moon, to shine in it: for the glory of God did lighten it, and the Lamb is the light thereof. [24] And the nations of them which are saved shall walk in the light of it: and the kings of the earth do bring their glory and honour into it. [25] And the gates of it shall not be shut at all by day: for there shall be no night there. [26] And they shall bring the glory and honour of the nations into it. [27] And there shall in no wise enter into it anything that_defileth, neither whatsoever worketh abomination, or maketh a lie: but they which are written in the Lamb's book of life."

Note

Jesus is the King of kings and Lord of lords: King of {kings and lords of the earth} and the "Nations" are "the people of God-Gentile/Ethnic People." In other words, all those who are not of the Twelve Tribes of Israel!

Revelation 22: 1-7 and 13-19 (KJV) says "And he shewed me a pure river of water of life, clear as crystal, proceeding out of the throne of God and of the Lamb. ² In the midst of the street of it, and on either side of the river, was there the tree of life, which bare twelve manner of fruits, and yielded her fruit every month: and the leaves of the tree were for the healing of the nations. ³ And there shall be no more curse: but the throne of God and of the Lamb shall be in it; and his servants shall serve him: ⁴ And they shall see his face; and his name shall be in their foreheads. ⁵ And there shall be no night there; and they need no candle, neither light of the sun; for the Lord God giveth them light: and they shall reign for ever and ever. ⁶ And he said unto me, These sayings are faithful and true: and the Lord God of the holy prophets sent his angel to shew unto his servants the things which must shortly be done. ⁷ Behold, I come quickly: blessed is he that keepeth the sayings of the prophecy of this book.

¹³ "I Am Alpha and Omega, the beginning and the end, the first and the last. ¹⁴ Blessed are they that do his commandments, that they may have right to the tree of life, and may enter in through the gates into the city. ¹⁵ For without are dogs, and sorcerers, and whoremongers, and murderers, and idolaters, and whosoever loveth and maketh a lie. ¹⁶ I Jesus have sent mine angel to testify unto you these things in the churches. I am the root and the offspring of David, and the bright and morning star. ¹⁷ And the Spirit and the bride say, Come. And let him that heareth say, Come. And let him that is athirst come. And whosoever will, let him take the water of life freely. ¹⁸ For I testify unto every man that heareth the words of the prophecy of this book, If any man shall add unto these things, God shall add unto him the plagues that are written in this book:"

SUMMARY

Now we will put it all together, look at the world today:

Rebellion, Revolution - Rebellion is open resistance to a government or authority; revolution is a rebellion that succeeds in overthrowing the government and establishing a new one. Revolution - the overthrow of a government by those who are governed.

Propaganda is one-sided communication designed to influence people's thinking and actions. A television commercial or a poster urging people to vote for a political candidate might be propaganda, depending on its method of persuasion. **(They use kids in their commercials) Have you notice every time they want to raise taxes... they use commercials for helping the kids. Etc.)**

Totalitarianism: The political idea that citizens should be totally and absolutely ruled by one party or group of people. No opposing views are tolerated.

One Worldism: One-Worldism and Globalism are one in the same: the belief that the government powers of the world should unite and center all their power within one authority. Personal liberty is severely limited under a fascist government. For example, the government limits travel to other countries and restricts any contact with their people. The government also controls the newspapers, radio, and other means of communication in its country. It issues propaganda to promote its policies, and it practices strict censorship to silence opposing views. All children are required to join youth organizations, where they exercise, march, and learn fascist beliefs. A secret police force crushes any resistance. Opposition may lead to imprisonment, torture, and death.

I believe I have written everything that I wanted to get across to You; the four words above with their definition I strongly believe is not what God winks at. As I stated in the "Forward" section of this book and I believe it needs to be a refresher to your mind now that you are at the end. The acronym (S.N.A.P.) stands for Satan Not About People; I use this because Satan wants is as many Souls to join him in the "Lake of Fire" right after the final judgement of God and *"GOD IS ABOUT TO DO HIS THING"* because this world and time we live in for the most part is going to hell in a hand basket. I believe the majority of the people who went on Satan's side during the First Earth age are living now—just look at all the wickedness that's going on. With that said, Ecclesiastes 1:9 (KJV) says "The thing that hath been, it is that which shall be; and that which is done is that which shall be done: and there is no new thing under the sun." I'll end this Book with what Jesus's half-brother said to the Twelve Tribes that are scattered aboard then and now, but most importantly for those who have turned from God and need to find their way back. I know Israel became a county again in 1948 which began the "Count-Down-of -The Hourglass," of the final generation of "The Figtree." Judah and Benjamin are the only tribes out of the twelve that inhabits Israel along with other nationalities especially the "Kenites." The other Ten Tribes after coming out of captivity they crossed the Caucasus Mountains and afterwards were called "Caucasian" when they moved into Europe and then crossed the Atlantic Ocean into Canada and the United States.

James 1: 1-7; 16-22 & 26-27 (KJV) says "James, a servant of God and of the Lord Jesus Christ, to the twelve tribes which are scattered abroad, greeting. [2] My brethren, count it all joy when ye fall into divers' temptations; [3] Knowing this, that the trying of your faith worketh patience. [4] But let patience have her perfect work, that ye may be perfect and entire, wanting nothing. [5] If any of you lack wisdom, let him ask of God, that giveth to all men liberally, and upbraideth not; and it shall be given him. [6] But let him ask in faith, nothing wavering. For he that wavereth is like a wave of the sea driven with the wind and tossed. [7] For let not that man think that he shall receive any thing of the Lord."

[16] "Do not err, my beloved brethren." [17] Every good gift and every perfect gift is from above, and cometh down from the Father of lights, with whom is no variableness, neither shadow of turning. [18] Of his own will begat he us with the word of truth, that we should be a kind of firstfruits of his creatures. [19] Wherefore, my beloved brethren, let every man be swift to hear, slow to speak, slow to wrath: [20] For the wrath of man worketh not the righteousness of God. [21] Wherefore lay apart all filthiness and superfluity of naughtiness, and receive with meekness the engrafted word, which is able to save your souls. [22] But be ye doers of the word, and not hearers only, deceiving your own selves."

[26] "If any man among you seem to be religious, and bridleth not his tongue, but deceiveth his own heart, this man's religion is vain.[27] Pure religion and undefiled before God and the Father is this, To visit the fatherless and widows in their affliction, and to keep himself unspotted from the world."

Remember when Moses asked God what His name is when the people ask who he talked too, God told Moses that His name is *"I Am That I Am"* (When you see LORD is in the Bible it is YHVH); The phrase *"I AM THAT I AM"* in the King James Version of the Bible in Hebrew language is (ehyeh asher ehyeh) and it derives from the Qal imperfect first-person form of the verb hayah: "I will be" and therefore indicates a connection between the name YHVH and being itself. YHVH is the source of all being and has being inherent in Himself (i.e., He is a necessary being). Everything else is a contingent being that derives existence from Him. The name YHVH also bespeaks the utter transcendence of God. In Himself, God is beyond Predications or Attributes of language: He is the source and foundation of all possibility of utterance and thus is beyond all definite descriptions.

Reference of Source: http://www.hebrew4christians.com.

APPENDIX

Books of the Bible and their Meaning (s)

THE OLD TESTSMENT		
The Law (Torah)/The Five Books of the Pentateuch		
Title	Meaning	Time Period
Genesis	"Bereshith"–In the Beginning	4,000 B.C.
Exodus	"veelleh shemoth - Redemption	1,446 B.C.
Leviticus	"vayyikra – Worship	1,445 B.C.
Numbers	"Bemidbar" – In the Wilderness	1,444 B.C.
Deuteronomy	"Haddebarim" – The Word	1, 406 B.C.

THE OLD TESTSMENT		
The History		
Joshua	"Yahsus" (Jesus) – Yahveh (GOD) the Savior	1,406 B.C.
Judges	"Shophetim" – Rulers	1,380 B.C.
Ruth	A Story of Loyalty	1,200 B.C.
I Samuel	"Shemuel" – Asked of God	1,105 B.C.
II Samuel		1,010 B.C.
I Kings	The Kingdom United	970 B.C.
II Kings	The Kingdom Divided	848 B.C.
I Chronicles	Dibrei hayyamim– Words of the Days	1,000 B.C.
II Chronicles		970 B.C.
Ezra	Born in Confusion	538 B.C.
Nehemiah	Comforter of Yahveh (GOD)	445 B.C.
Esther	"Estthur" – The Hidden Star	479 B.C.
Job	"Iyyob" – Persecuted	2,000 B.C.
Psalms	"Tehillim" – Songs, to Rejoice	1,000 B.C.
Proverbs	"Mishlai" – To Rule	970 B.C.
Ecclesiastes	"Koheleth" – The Preacher	940 B.C.
Song of Soloman	"Shir Hashshirim"– Songs of Songs	970 B.C.
Isaiah	Salvation of Yahveh (GOD)	740 B.C.
Jeremiah	Launches Forth	626 B.C.
Lamentations	One God Sends Forth	586 B.C.

THE OLD TESTSMENT		
History		
Ezekiel	"Yehezkel" – El is Strong	1,446 B.C.
Daniel	GOD my Judge	605 B.C.

THE OLD TESTSMENT		
The Minor Prophets		
Title	Meaning	Time Period
Hosea	"Hoshea" – Salvation	750 B.C.
Joel	Yahveh (GOD) is GOD	835 B.C.
Amos	Burden	760 B.C.
Obadiah	Servant of Yahveh (GOD)	855 B.C.
Jonah	Warmth of a Dove	785 B.C.
Micah	Who is like Yahveh (GOD)?	740 B.C.
Nahum	The Compassionate, or Consoler	620 B.C.
Habakkuk	To Embrace	605 B.C.
Zephaniah	Hidden of Yahveh (GOD)	635 B.C.
Haggai	Feast of Festival	520 B.C.
Zechariah	Remembered of Yahveh (GOD)	520 B.C.
Malachi	My Messenger	440 B.C.

THE NEW TESTSMENT		
The Four Gospels		
Title	Meaning	Time Period
Matthew	Jesus, The True King	6 B.C.
Mark	Jesus, The Servant of All	26 A.D.
Luke	Jesus, The Man of Compassion	6 B.C.
John	Jesus, The Son of God	26 A.D.
Acts	The Acts of the Apostles	30 A.D.
The Epistles		
Romans	God's Plan to Save Mankind	57 A.D.
I Corinthians	The Problems of the Church in Corinth	55 A.D.
II Corinthians	Paul Answers His Accusers	56 A.D.
Galatians	Christianity as a Reality, not "Traditions"	49 A.D.
Ephesians	We are One in Christ	60 A.D.

THE NEW TESTSMENT		
The Epistles		
Title	Meaning	Time Period
Philippians	Serve Others with Joy	61 A.D.
Colossians	Jesus is Above All Things	60 A.D.
I Thessalonians	Encouragement for New Christians	51 A.D.
II Thessalonians	The Return of Christ	52 A.D.
I Timothy	Advice to a Young Preacher	64 A.D.
II Timothy	Encouragement to a Soldier of Christ	66 A.D.
Titus	Instructions for Doing Good	64 A.D.
Philemon	A Slave becomes a Christian	60 A.D.
Hebrews	A Better Life through Christ	66 A.D.
James	How to Live as a Christian	49 A.D.
I Peter	Written to God's Elect	62 A.D.
II Peter	Correcting False Teachings	67 A.D.
I John	The Lover of God	90 A.D.
II John	Beware of the False Teachers	90 A.D.

THE NEW TESTSMENT		
III John	Love to those who Walk in the Truth	90 A.D.
Jude	Warnings of Evil Men and False Teachers	65 A.D.
	The Apocalypse	
Revelations	"apokalupsis"–to Reveal, Prophesy	95 A.D.

Where to Find the 7 Seals, Trumps & Vails

Number	Seals	Trumps	Vails
1	Rev. 6: 1	Rev. 8: 7	Rev. 16: 2
2	Rev. 6: 3	Rev. 8: 8	Rev. 16: 3
3	Rev. 6: 5	Rev. 8: 10	Rev. 16: 4
4	Rev. 6: 7	Rev. 8: 12	Rev. 16: 8
5	Rev. 6: 9	Rev. 9: 1	Rev. 16: 10
6*	Rev. 6: 12	Rev. 9: 13	Rev. 16: 12
7**	Rev 8: 1	Rev. 11: 15	Rev. 16: 17

NOTE:

The asterisks indicate 6-6-6 (number of man) the time frame and events that happen when Satan will appear in "body" form as a supernatural being, claiming to be Jesus Christ, but instead is "The Anti-Christ." Most importantly is 7-7-7 (Spiritual Perfection) when Jesus Christ comes back as the Messiah (King of kings and Lord of lords. The Seals are not in chronology order, but when 6-6-6 happens the Seals, Trumps and Vails are chronology.

We are now in the Fifth Seal (Teaching to Seal the Hearts and Minds)!

Frequently Used Words and their Meanings! Reference: *"The New Strong's Expanded Exhausted Concordance of the Bible Red Letter Edition"* (Hebrew and Aramaic, Greek Dictionary)

(1) **Abomination:** Hebrew # 8251 shiqquwts (shik-koots'); or shiqquts (shik-koots'); from #8262; disgusting, i.e. filthy; especially idolatrous or (concretely) an idol: Strong's #946 bddugma (bdel '- oog-mah); from #948: detestation, i.e. (Specially) idolatry:

(2) **Adam:** Hebrew #120 'Adam (aw-daw m'); from #1 19; ruddy i.e. a human being (an individual or the species, mankind, etc.): #119 'Adam (aw-dam'): to show blood (in the face), i.e. flush or tum rosy. NOTE: Adam without the article is man in general, *The Adam* in (Gen. 2:7, 8, and 15 [first occurrence]) is with the article and particle, and it's a very emphatic Hebrew word for Adam ("eth-Ha'adham = *"this same man Adam"*). Article in English terms a, an, and the; Particle in English terms is one of a class of forms, as prepositions or conjunctions, consisting of a single word that has no inflection:

(3) **Again:** Hebrew # 3254 yacaph (yaw-af); a primitive root; to add or augment (often adverbial, to continue to do a thing). Jesus uses "Again" in (John 3:3 & 7) Greek # 509 - anothen, an'-o-then; from #507 ; from above; by anal - from the first; by implication Anew: from above, again, from the beginning (very first), the top; from #473 upward or on the top: above, brim, high, up:

(4) **Air:** {1 Th. 4:17} Greek #109 aer (ah-ayr'); from aemi (to breathe unconsciously, i.e. respire; by anal. to blow); "air' (as naturally circumambient [Enclosing!]: - air. Comp. #5594 - psucho (psoo'-kho) a primitive verb; to breathe (voluntarily but gently; thus, differing on the one hand from #4154, which denotes prop. a forcible respiration; and on the other from the base of #109, which refers prop. to an inanimate breeze), i.e. (by impl. Of reduction of temperature by evaporation) to chill (fig): - wax cold.

(5) **Amber:** Hebrew #2830 chashmal (khash-mal'); of uncertain derivation; probably bronze or polished spectrum metal:

(6) **Angels:** Hebrew #4397 mal'ak (mal-aw k'); from an unused root meaning to dispatch as a deputy a messenger; specifically, of God, i.e. an angel (also a prophet, priest or teacher):

(7) **Began:** Hebrew #2490 [Gen. 4:26]chalal, (khaw-lal'): a primitive root [comp. #2470]; prop. To bore, i.e. (by impl.) to wound, to dissolve; fig. To profane (a person, place or thing), to break (one's word), to begin (as if by an "opening wedge"); denom. (from #2485) to play (the flute):

(8) **Beguiled:** Hebrew # 5377 nasha '(naw-shaw'); a primitive root; to lead astray, i.e. (mentally) to delude, or (morally) to seduce: Greek #1818 exapatao (ex-ap-at-ah'-o); from #1537 and #538; to seduce wholly: (*II Cor. 11: 3*)

(9) **Beryl:** Hebrew # 8658 tarshiysh (tar-sheesh'); probably of foreign derivation [compare #8659]; a gem, perhaps the topaz:

(10) **Branch:** Hebrew # 5342 netser (nay' -tser); from 5341 in the sense of greenness as a striking color; a shoot; figuratively, a descendant: #5341 natsar (naw-tsar'); a primitive root; to guard, in a good sense (to protect, maintain, obey, etc.) or a bad one {to conceal, etc.):

(11) **Breath:** Hebrew #5397 neshamah (ne.sh-aw-maw '); from #5395; a puff, i.e. wind, angry or vital breath, divine inspiration, intellect, or (concretely) an animal: #5397 blast, (that) breathe (-eth), inspiration, soul, spirit:

(12) **Brightness:** Hebrew #5051 nogahh (no'-gah); from #5050; brilliancy (literally or figuratively): #5050 nagahh (naw-gah'); a prime root; to glitter; causatively, to illuminate:

(13) **Cloven:** Greek # 1266 διαμεριζω {12x} diamerizo, *dee-am-er-is-mos', from 1223 to 3307; to partition thoroughly* (lit. in distribution, fig. in dissension): - cloven {1x}, divide {5x}, part {6x}Note: Simplified–Goes out in many directions–In Acts 2:3 the language that was spoken went out in every language/tongue and dialect that was there so it could be understood.

(14) **Conception:** Hebrew #2032 herown (hay-rone'); or herayown (hay-raw-yone'); from #2029; pregnancy; Hebrew #2029 harah (haw-raw'); a primitive root; to be (or become) pregnant, conceive (literally or figuratively):

(15) **Converted:** Greek #4762 strepho (stref'-o); strengthened from the base of#5157; to twist, i.e. turn quite around or reverse (literally or fig.):

(16) **Corruption:** Greek #5356 phthora (fthor-ah'); from #5351; decay, i.e. ruin (spontaneous or inflicted, literally or figuratively):

(17) **Damnation:** Greek #2920 krisis (kree'-sis); decision (subjectively or objectively, for or against); by extension, a tribunal; by implication, justice (especially, divine law):

(18) **Darkness:** Hebrew #2822 choshek (kho-shek'); from #2821; the dark; hence (literally) darkness; figuratively, misery, destruction, death, ignorance, sorrow, wickedness:

(19) **Devil:** Greek #1228 diabolos (dee-ab-ol-os); from 1225; a traducer; specially, Satan [compare #7854]: #1225 diaballo {dee-ab- al'-lo); from #1223 and #960; (figuratively) to traducer: #7854 satan (saw-tawn'); from #7853; an opponent; especially (with the article prefixed) Satan, the archenemy of good: #7853 satan (saw-tan'); a primitive root; to attack, (figuratively) accuse:

(20) **Dragon:** Greek #1404 drakon (drak'-own); probably from an alternate form of derkomai (to look); a fabulous kind of serpent (perhaps as supposed to fascinate):

(21) **Earth:** Hebrew #776 'erets (eh'-rets); from an un used root probably meaning to be firm; the earth (at large, or partitively a land): Greek #1093 ge (ghay); contracted from a primary word; soil; by extension a region, or the solid part or the whole of the terrene globe {including the occupants in each application):

(22) **Eat:** Hebrew # 398 'akal (aw-kal'); a prime root; to eat (lit. or fig.): #8378 ta'avah (tah-av-aw '): from #183 (abbreviated); a longing; by implication, a delight (subjectively, satisfaction, objectively, a charm): #183 'avah (aw-vaw'); a primitive root; to wish for: covet, (greatly) desired, be desirous, long, lust (after).

(23) **Enemy:** Greek #2190 echthro (ech-thros'); from a primary echtho (to hate); hateful (passively, odious, or actively, hostile); usually as a noun, an adversary (especially Satan):

(24) **Enmity:** Hebrew #342 'eybah (ay-baw'); from #340; hostility: #340 'ayab (aw-yab'); a primitive root; to hate (as one of an opposite tribe or party); hence to be hostile:

(25) **Field:** Hebrew #7704 sadeh (saw-deh'); or saday (saw-dah'- ee); from an unused root meaning to spread out; a field (as flat):

(26) **Finished:** Hebrew #3615 sadeh (saw-deh'); a primitive root; to end, whether intransitive (to cease, be finished, perish) or transitived (to complete, prepare, consume):

(27) **Formed:** Hebrew #3335 yatsar (yaw-tsar'); probably identical with #3334 (through the squeezing into shape); ([compare #3331]); to mould into a form; especially as a potter; fig., to determine (i.e. form a resolution):

(28) **Foundation:** Greek #2602 katabole (kat-ab-ol-ay'); from #2598; a deposition, i.e. founding; fig., conception: #2598 kataballo (kat-ab-al'-lo) from #2596 and #906; to throw down:

(29) **Generation:** Greek #1081 gennema (ghen'-nay-mah): from #1080; offspring; by analogy, produce (literally or figuratively): #1080 gennao (ghen-nah'-o); from a variation of # 1085; to procreate (properly, of the father, but by extension of the mother); figuratively, lo regenerate: # 1085 genos (ghen'-os); from # 1096; "kin" (abstract or concrete, literal or figurative, individual or collective): *Hebrew #8435* towledah (to-led-aw'); or toledah (to-led- aw'); from # 3205; (plural only) descent, i.e. family; (figuratively) history:

(30) **Ground:** Hebrew #127 'adamah (ad-aw-maw'); from #1 19; soil (from its general redness):

(31) **Hell:** Greek # 1067 geena (gheh'-en-nah); of Hebrew origin [1516 and 2011]; valley of (the son of) Hinnom; ge-henna (or Ge-Hinnom), a valley of Jerusalem, used (figuratively) as a name for the place (or state) of everlasting punishment: *Hebrew #7585* showl (sheh-ole'); or shol (sheh-ole'); from #7592; hades or the world of the dead (as if a subterranean retreat), include. Its accessories and inmates: grave, hell, pit.

(32) **Image:** Hebrew#6754 tselem (tseh'-lem); from an unused root meaning to shade; a phantom, i.e. (figuratively) illusion, resemblance; hence, a representative figure, especially an idol:

(33) **Incorruption:** Greek #861 aphthrsia (af-thar-see'-ah); from #862; incorruptibility; genitive case unending existence; (figuratively) genuineness:

(33) **Kenite: (ken'-ite) (6) See Kenites.** A member of a Canaanite tribe. Hebrew #7014 Qayin (kah'-yin); the same as #7013 (with a play upon the affinity to #7069); Kajin, the name of the first child, also of a place in Palestine, and of an Oriental tribe: - Cain, Kenite (-s). #7017 Qeyniy, (Kay-nee'); or Qiyniy {J Chron. 2:55}, (Kee-nee'); patron from #7014; a Kenite or member of the tribe of Kajin: - Kenite.

(34) **Likeness:** Hebrew #1823 demuwth (dem-ooth'); from #1819; resemblance; concretely model, shape; adverbially, like: # 1819 damah (daw-maw'); a primitive root; to compare; by implication, to resemble, liken, consider:

(35) **Lust:** Hebrew #1939 epithumia (ep-ee-thoomee'); from #1937; a longing (especially for what is forbidden):

(36) **Manna:** Hebrew # 4478 man (mawn): from #4100; literally, a whatness (so to speak), i.e. manna (so called from the question about it. Greek #3131 manna (man'-nah); of Hebrew origin [#4478]; manna (i.e. man), an edible gum:

(37) **Mark:** Hebrew #226 'owth (oth); probably from #225 (in the sense of appearing); a signal (literally or figuratively}, as a t1ag, beacon, monument, omen, prodigy, evidence, etc.:

(38) **Moved:** Hebrew #7363 rachaph (raw-khaf'); a primitive root; to brood; by implication, to be relaxed:

(39) **Natural:** Greek #5591 psuchikos (psoo-khee-kos'); from #5590; sensitive, i.e. animate (in distinction on the one hand from #4152, which is the higher or renovated nature; and on the other from #5446, which is the lower or bestial nature:

(40) **Perdition:** Greek #684 apoleia (ap-o'-Ii-a); from a presumed derivative of #622; ruin or loss (physical, spiritual or eternal): #622 apollumi (ap-ol'-loo-mee); from #575 and the base of #3639; to destroy fully (reflexively, to perish, or lose), literally or figuratively:

(41) **Repentance:** Greek #3341 metanoia (met-an'-oy-ah); from #3340; (subjectively) compunction (for guilt, including reformation); by implication reversal ([of] another's] decision): #3340 metanoeo (met-an-o-eh'o); from #3326 and #3539; to think differently or afterwards, i.e. reconsider (morally, feel compunction):

(42) **Satan:** Greek # 4567 Satanas (sat-an-as'); of Chaldee origin corresponding to #4566 (with the def. affix); the accuser, i.e. the devil: - Satan #4566 Satan (sat- an'); of *Hebrew* origin [#7854; Satan, i.e. the devil: - Satan. Comp. #4567.

(43) **Seal:** Greek #4972 sphragizo (sfrag-id' -zo); from #4973; to stamp (with a signet or private mark) for security or preservation (lit. or fig.); by implication, to keep secret, to attest:

(44) **Seed:** Hebrew # 2233 zera' (zeh' -rah); from #2232; seed; figuratively, fruit, plant, sowing- time, posterity: #2232 zara' (zaw-rah'); a primitive root; to sow; fig., to disseminate, plant, fructify: *Greek #4690* sperma (sper' mah); from #4687; something sown, i.e. seed (including the male "sperm") by implication, offspring, specifically, a remnant (fig., as if kept over for planting):

(45) **Serpent:** Hebrew #5175 nachash (naw-khawsh'); from #5172; a snake (from its hiss): #5172 nachash (naw-khash'); a primitive root; properly, to hiss, i.e. whisper a (magic) spell; generally, to prognosticate: Greek #3789 ophis (of '-is); probably from #3700 (through the ideal of sharpness of vision); a snake, figuratively (as a type of sly cunning) an artful malicious person, especially Satan:

(46) **Soul:** Hebrew #5315 nephesh (neh '-fesh); from #5314; prop. a breathing creature, i.e. animal or (abstr.) vitality; used very widely in a literally accommodated or figurative sense (bodily or mental): - any, appetite, beast, body, breath, creature, will: #5314 naphash (naw-fash'); a primitive root; to breathe; passive, to be breathed upon, i.e. (fig.) refreshed (as if by a current of air): - (be) refresh selves (-ed).

(47) **Spirit:** Hebrew #7307 ruwach (roo'-akh); from #7306; wind; by resemblance breath, i.e. a sensible (or even violent) exhalation; fig., life, anger, unsubstantiality; by extension. a region of the sky; by resemblance spirit, but only of a rational being (incl. Its expression & functions):

(48) **Spiritual:** Greek #4152 pneumatikos (pnyoo-mat-ik-os'); from #4151; non- carnal, i.e. (humanly) ethereal (as opposed to gross), or (demoniacally) a spirit (concretely), or (divinely) supernatural, regenerate, religious: Compare #5591. #4151 pneuma (pnyoo'-mah); from #4154; a current of air, i.e. breath (blast) or a breeze; by analogy or figuratively, a spirit, i.e. (human) the rational soul (by implication) vital principle, mental disposition, etc., or (superhuman) an angel, demon, or (divine) God, Christ's spirit, the Holy Spirit: Compare #5590.

(49) **Tares:** Greek #2215 **zizanion** (dziz-an' -ee-on); of uncertain origin; darnel or false grain:

(50) **Till:** Hebrew #5647 **'abad** (aw-bad'); a primitive root: to work (in any sense); by implication, to serve, till, (causatively) enslave. etc.:

(51) **Tongue:** Greek # 1100 γλῶσσα {50x} **glŏssa,** *gloce-sah';* of uncert. aff.; the *tongue;* by impl. a *language* (spec., one naturally unacquired): NOTE: Is a language(s) [A foreign or strange language which one has not learned, but yet is enabled to speak as a result of the supernatural intervention of the Holy Spirit, particularly in what the New Testament (N.T.) calls the Baptism in the Holy Spirit by Jesus Christ. **Only Three Biblical Historic Events**: Speaking in Foreign Tongues and Dialects: (1) *Pentecost–*Acts 2:3-11; (2) *Gentiles* -at Caesarea in Acts 10:46 and (3) *Disciples of John the Baptist–*at Ephesus in Acts 19: 6. These were all languages unknown to the Speakers, spoken at that particular time in demonstration of them being baptized into the body of Jesus Christ (I Corinthians 12:13).

(52) **Touch:** Hebrew #5060 **naga'** {naw–gah'); a primitive root; properly, to touch, i.e. lay the hand upon (for any purpose; euphcm ... to lie with a woman): by implication, to reach (figuratively, to arrive, acquire); violently, to strike (punish, defeat, destroy, etc.):

(53) **Transformed:** Greek #3345 metaschematizo tmet-askh-ay- mat-id'-zo); from #3326 and a derivative of #4976; to transfigure or disguise; figuratively, to apply (by accommodation):

(54) **Tree:** {Gen. 2:9} Hebrew #6086 ets (ates); from #6095; a tree (from its firmness); hence wood (plural sticks): #6095 atsah (aw-tsaw'); a primitive root; prop. to fasten (or make firm), i.e. to close (the eyes): - shut.

(55) **Tyrus:** Hebrew #6865 Tsor (tsore); or Tsowr (tsore); the same as #6864 a rock; Tsor, a place in Palestine: Tyre, Tyrus. ***. tsur. See #6697. #6864 tsor (tsore); from #6696; a stone (as if pressed hard or to a point); (by implication or use) a knife:

(56) **Void:** Hebrew #922 bohuw (bo'-hoo); from an unused root (meaning to be empty); a vacuity, i.e. (superficially) an undistinguishable ruin:

(58) **Was:** Hebrew #1961 hayah (haw-yaw '); a primitive root [comp. 1933); to exist, i.e. be or become, come to pass (always emphatic, and not a mere copula or auxiliary): - beacon, altogether, he (-come); accomplished, committed, like), break, cause, come (to pass), continue, do, faint, fall, + follow, happen, have, last, pertain, quit (one-) self, require, use.

(59) **Wings:** Hebrew #3671 kanaph (kaw-nawf); from #3670; an edge or extremity; specifically (of a bird or army) a wing, (of a garment or bed clothing) a flap, (of the earth) a quarter, (of a building) a pinnacle: #3670 kanaph (kaw-naf); a primitive root; properly, to project laterally, i.e. probably (reflexive) to withdraw:

(60) **Without, Form**: Hebrew #8414 tohuw (to'-hoo); from an unused root meaning to lay waste; a desolation (of surface), i.e. desert; figuratively, a worthless thing; adverbially, in vain:

The Spiritual Significance of Numbers

"The Companion Bible" (KJV) <u>Appendix 10</u>

<u>One</u> - Denotes Unity, and Commencement. The first occurrences of words or utterances denote their essential significance, in interpretation. First Day, Light.

<u>Two</u> - Denotes Difference. If two different persons agree in testimony, it is conclusive. Otherwise two implies opposition, enmity, and division, as was the work of the Second day.

<u>Three</u> - Denotes Completeness, as three lines complete perfection and completeness.

<u>Four</u> - Denotes Creative Works (3+1), and always has reference to the material creation, as pertaining to the earth, and things "under the sun," and things terrestrial.

<u>Five</u> - Denotes Divine Grace. It is (4+1). It's God adding His gifts and blessing to the works of His hands. It's the leading factor in the Tabernacle measurements.

<u>Six</u> - Denotes the Human Number. Man was; created on the sixth day; and was the first occurrence of the number makes it (and all multiples of it) the hall-mark of all connected with man. He works six days. The hours of His day are a multiple of six.

<u>Seven</u> - Denotes Spiritual Perfection. I t is the number or hall-mark of the Holy Spirit work. He is the Author of God's Word, and seven is stamped on it as the water-mark is seen in the manufacture of paper. He is the Author and Giver of life; and seven is the number, which regulates every period of Incubation and Gestation, in insects, birds, animals, and man.

<u>Eight</u> - Denotes Resurrection, Regeneration; a new beginning or commencement. The eighth is a new first. It is the number that has to do with the Lord, Who rose on the eighth or new "first-day. "This, therefore,

the (Dominical Number - Of or associated with Christ as the Lord; and relating to Sunday ac; the Lord's Day.)

Nine - Denotes Finality of Judgement. It is (3X3), the product of Divine Completeness. The number nine, or its factors or multiples are seen in all cases when judgement is the subject.

Ten - Denotes Ordinal Perfection. Another new first; after the ninth digit, when numeration commences anew.

Eleven - Denotes Disorder, Disorganization, because it is one short of the number twelve (see below).

Twelve - Denotes Government Perfection. It is the number or factor of all numbers connected with government: whether by Tribes or Apostles, or in measurements of time, or in things which have to do with government in the heavens and earth.

Thirteen - Denotes Rebellion, Apostasy, Defection, Disintegration, and Revolution. The first occurrence fixes this (Gen. 14 4); and the second confirms it (Gen. 17:25).

Seventeen -Denotes a combination of Spiritual and Order (10 + 7). It is the seventh prime number (13 is the sixth prime number).

NOTE: Other numbers follow the Law which governs the smaller numbers, as being their Factors, Sums, Products or Multiples: e.g.

$24 = (12 \times 2)$ A higher form of 12.

$25 = 5^2$ Grace Intensified

$27 = 3^3$ Divinity Intensified

$28 = 7 \times 4$ Spiritual Perfection in connection with the Earth

30 = 3 x 10   Divine Perfection applied to Order

40 = 10 x 4   Divine Order applied to earthly things. Hence, the number of Probation.

The Four Perfect Numbers: **3, 7, 10** and 12, have for their product the remark number **2,520**. It is the Least Common: Multiple of the ten digits governing all numeration; and can, therefore, be divided by each of the nine digits, without a remainder. It is the number of Chronological Perfection (**7 x 360**) = **2,520**.

GLOSSARY

A. <u>Asili</u>: Is the developmental germ/seed or *DNA* of a culture.

B. <u>Black People (Blacks)</u>: 1) To an Eurocentric and most Americans, they are careless of their own life and that of others, kills willingly for the sake of killing, bad, non-gifted, non-intelligent beings, and inferior to all other races.

*2) They are an ethnic group of people who skin color happens to be of dark complexion, black, brown, or light brown. In some circles it is known that they are the first human being to be here on earth, but since history has been distorted by the White Man that will never fly in this country because of their image for themselves.

C. <u>Elitism</u>: Is the system in which the Elites rule over because of their economic wealth in the country they have influence over. **Note:** I often refer to the Elites as Whites or White People.

D. <u>Eurocentrism</u>: Is both the Hellenic and Hebraic modes of Plato's ideology and centered or focused on Europe and Europeans.

E. <u>Depression/ Oppression</u>: [a] Depression: A psychoneurotic or psychotic disorder marked especially by sadness, inactivity, and difficulty in thinking and concentration, **[b.] Oppression: (1)** Unjust or cruel exercise of authority or power**, (2)** A sense of being weighed down in body and, or mind.

F. Dichotomization: The splitting of the phenomenon into confrontational conflicting parts.

G. Dominant/Domination: [a.] Dominant: Commanding, controlling, or prevailing over others, [b.] Domination:

(1) Supremacy or preeminence over another, (2) Exercise of mastery or preponderant influence.

H. Hidden & Public Transcripts: [a.] Hidden Transcript (s): They are either written or silent, but they mostly resist against whatever public transcript (s) it may go against. [b.] Public Transcripts: Transcript (s) that are made available for the public and some are official, and some are unofficial. **Example:** Official Transcripts are written laws, and Unofficial Transcripts are newspapers.

I. Ideology: The body of ideals reflecting the social needs and aspirations of an individual, groups, class, or culture.

J. Objectification: Is a cognitive modality, which appoints everything other than the self as the object.

K. Politics: (1) Political, (2) Characterized by shrewdness in managing, contriving, or dealing, (3) Sagacious in promoting a policy, (4) Shrewdly tactful in getting things done.

L. Race: (1) A family, tribe, people, or nation belonging to the same stock, (2) A class or kind of people unified by a community of interest, habits, or characteristics, (3) A division of mankind possessing traits that are transmissible by decent and sufficient to characterize it as a distinct human type. * My interpretation of Acts 17:26 (KJV) "And hath made of one blood all nations of men for dwelling on all the face of the earth, and hath determined the times before appointed, and the bounds of their habitation;" there's only one race, the human race, because we all were formed from the earth. **Note:** Hath made of one blood refers to the Atoning Blood of Christ who die for all mankind that they may have Eternal Life with Him in the Kingdom of God!

M. *__Racism:__* Prejudice against those who do not have the economical and wealth which equal real power and authority. The color of a person's skin is secondary but put first in the minds of the less fortunate is that it's the notion that one's own ethnicity is superior to another.

N. *__Resistance:__* An opposing or retarding force that may engage in sabotage and, or secret operations against occupation forces and collaborators.

O. __Rhetorical Ethics:__ Is the culturally structured European hypocrisy that says things that it has no intention in doing. *A state of being stagnant in its actions.

P. __Utamawazo:__ Is the culturally structured thought pattern that its member (s) must have if the *Asili* is to be fulfilled.

Q. __Utamaroho:__ Is the vital force or trust of energy of a culture that's set-in motion by the *Asili*.

R. *__White People (Whites):__* They think they are God's gift to humanity, and without them there could be no civilization because of their intelligence and superior to others. Whiteness is central to the European self-image of *good* and beautiful. Caucasians on the other hand I refer to the *masses* of people, because they have been hoodwinked by the Elites.

Note:

The original Caucasians are those who were born and or lived in the Caucasus region and known as Peoples of the Caucasus. The peoples of the Caucasus are diverse making up more than fifty ethnic groups throughout the Caucasus region. When the ten northern tribes of Israel known as the "Ten Lost Tribes" crossed that mountain and came into Europe, the Europeans Whites/Elites called them Caucasians. Caucasian is sometimes used to refer to: White People in general and especially in the United States Caucasians are considered as White Americans, non-Hispanic and non-Black. The difference between White and Caucasians is because a Caucasian can be white depending on the skin tone, but a white person will never be called a Caucasian. In doing a comparison of the two people, Caucasian is considered the larger race while the white is the smaller one. In the United States most people have been using these terms in place of the other, that has always been a misconception although it is on the census as such.

REFERENCES

The Scripture quotations marked KJV are from the King James Bible (Authorized Version). First Published in 1611. Quoted from the KJV Classic Reference Bible, Copyright © 1983 by The Zondervan Corporation.

Study References:

(1) **"The Companion Bible"** The Authorized Version of 1611 King James Bible with the Structures and Critical, Explanatory and Suggestive Notes with 198 Appendixes; by E. W. Bullinger-King James Version published in 1990 by Kregel Publications, a division of Kregel, Inc. P. O. Box 2607, Grand Rapids, Michigan 49501: ISBN 0-8254-2179-9 (Burgundy bounded leather, indexed) Printed in Great Britain.

(2) **"The New Strong's Expanded Exhausted Concordance of the Bible Red Letter Edition"** by James Strong, L.L.D., S.T.D; (Thomas Nelson Publishers since 1798). BS425.S845 2001 2001032651 220.5'2033-dc21 Printed in China. NOTE: Takes the English word (s) back to its "Original Language" {Hebrew & Greek} with its definition (s).

(3) **"Vine's Complete Expositor Dictionary of Old and New Testament Words with Topical Index"** (Keyed to Strong's Reference Numbers). By W.E. Vine, Merrill F. Unger, William White Jr. Thomas Nelson Publishers since 1798; ISBN 978-0-7852-1160-0

{1. Bible-Dictionaries I. Title BS440.S746 1996 96-8956220.3- dc20 CIP} Printed in the United States of America **34 - 10**

(4) "Smith's Biblical Dictionary" By William Smith, L.L.D.; Revised and edited by F. N. and M. A. Peloubet; Nelson Reference & Electronic (A division of Thomas Nelson Publishers since 1798). [BS 440.S6 1982] 220.0 86-5281; ISBN 0-8407-5542-2 and ISBN 0-8407-3085-3 (pbk.)

(5) "The Interlinear Hebrew-Greek- English Bible" (Coded with Strong's Concordance Numbers)Four-Volume Edition by J.P. Green, Sr. {General Editor and Translator} Copyright © 1976, 1977,1978, 1979, 1980, 1981, 1984 Second Edition © 1985 (Sovereign Grace Publishers); I.S.B.N. 1-878442-00-7–Complete: Four Volume Bible; I.S.B.N. 1-878442-01-5–Three Volume Old Testament. **Note:** This is the closest Bible in print taken from the "Masoretes," The goal of the Masoretes was to guard and preserve the text of the Hebrew Bible, which had been handed down from generation to generation.

Printed in the United States
By Bookmasters